Time Management

About the series

Your Personal Trainer is a series of five books designed to help you learn, or develop, key business skills. Fun, flexible and involving (and written by experienced, real-life trainers), each title in the series acts as your very own 'personal fitness trainer', allowing you to focus on your own individual experience and identify priorities for action.

Assertiveness   1 904298 13 3
Stress Management 1 904298 17 6
Interviewing Skills   1 904298 14 1
Negotiating Skills   1 904298 15 X
Time Management   1 904298 16 8

Time Management

by Debra Allcock Tyler

First published in 2003 by
Spiro Press
17-19 Rochester Row
London SW1P 1LA
Telephone: +44 (0)870 400 1000

ISBN 1 904298 16 8

British Library Cataloguing-in-Publication Data.
A catalogue record for this book is available from the British Library.

Library of Congress Cataloging-in-Publication. Data on file.

Series devised by: Astrid French and Susannah Lear
Series Editor: Astrid French

Spiro Press USA
3 Front Street
Suite 331
PO Box 338
Rollinsford NH 03869
USA

Typeset by: Q3 Digital/Litho, Queens Road, Loughborough
Printed in Great Britain by: Cromwell Press
Cover image by: PhotoDisc
Cover design by: Cachet Creatives

Contents

Introduction   vii

How to use this book   ix

Fitness Assessment   1
Test your current skills fitness

Managing your work   5
1 Attitude   5
2 Priorities   6
3 Tasks   8

Managing people   12
4 People   12
5 Meetings   14
6 Interruptions   16

Getting a life   18
7 Balancing life   18
8 Managing stress   20

Fitness Profile   23
Strengths and weaknesses identified

Managing your work   27
1 Attitude   27
2 Priorities   29
3 Tasks   32

Managing people   40
4 People   40
5 Meetings   43
6 Interruptions   47

Getting a life   50
7 Balancing life   50
8 Managing stress   53

How good are you at time management?   59

Warm-up   61

Work-out   63
Activities and exercises to build your fitness

Managing your work   67
1 Attitude   67
2 Priorities   71
3 Tasks   76

Managing people   84
4 People   84
5 Meetings   89
6 Interruptions   95

Getting a life   99
7 Balancing life   99
8 Managing stress   103

Keeping Fit   111

Further Reading   117

Introduction

Welcome to *Time Management,* part of a brand new series – **Your Personal Trainer** – which offers you an exciting new way to learn, or develop, key business skills. Fun, flexible and involving, each title in this series acts as your very own 'personal fitness trainer', allowing you to focus on your individual experience and identify priorities for action.

Designed as a self-development workbook, each title creates an individual record of what you have achieved.

This book focuses on developing your *time management* skills. Most of us have too much to do and not enough time to do it in, and not just at work. We have to juggle our home lives, social commitments and families as well as fit in any extras such as exercise, study or evening classes. Never mind any leisure time! This book will give you an opportunity to assess where you are now and then take you through some 'exercises' to get you to where you want to be.

> *WATCH OUT FOR YOUR TRAINER*
> He will give you tips and alert you to potential problems as you work your way through the book.

There are no magic solutions – like any real exercise programme, getting 'fit' in time management takes commitment, practice and then simply sticking with it.

What is effective time management?

Why is it that some people, no matter how many time management courses they go on, or how much help they receive, never seem to get any better at managing their time? And yet other people seem to take on more and more work and get it done? Is it really simply down to competence? Is effective time management an innate trait that has nothing to do with learning and everything to do with being genetically 'programmed' to be either good or bad at managing time?

You will get the most out of this book if you work through it systematically, checking up on your time management skills from 1-8. This will enable you to get a good overall view of your fitness.

However, you may choose to focus on a particular area of skill (eg Managing people), working through the relevant section in Fitness Assessment, then moving on to subsequent sections in Fitness Profile and Work-out. These sections are clearly identified in the text, with directions to follow-up reading marked with an arrow *at the end of each section*.

Finally, if you want a quick review of key learning points, check out the summary checklists at the end of each section in Work-out.

Whichever way you choose to use this book, enjoy the experience!

Fitness Assessment

Managing your work

Your attitude to work, and how well you organize it, affects how time efficient you are. The following three assessments focus on managing your work.

ASSESSMENT 1: ATTITUDE

How you view your work and life, and the things that you have to do within them, has an enormous impact on your ability to be effective and achieve what you want. Feeling positive about your own abilities, the amount you have to do and the support available is half the battle towards managing time effectively.

Complete the following questionnaire to assess your attitude to your work and life.
Tick the response that is the closest to describing how you feel.

1   When thinking about managing my time
    A   I always feel completely out of control.   ☐
    B   I occasionally feel in control.   ☐
    C   I usually feel in control.   ☐

2   When thinking about my work
    A   I don't much care what happens.   ☐
    B   I care so much that I get stressed.   ☐
    C   I feel excited and interested.   ☐

3   I believe that work is
    A   Key to feeling worthwhile.   ☐
    B   A means of getting money.   ☐
    C   An interruption to real life.   ☐

4 When I have too much to do
   A I see it as a challenge. ☐
   B I get angry and frustrated. ☐
   C I become less able to deliver. ☐

5 I think that
   A Every task should be completed to the highest quality. ☐
   B Every task should be completed to a minimum standard. ☐
   C Some tasks should be completed to a high quality and some not done at all. ☐

ASSESSMENT 2: PRIORITIES

This assessment will help you establish how clear you are about your priorities, and if you have enough information to make the right decisions. Good decisions about priorities are highly dependent on clarity about job role, responsibilities and key result areas.

Look at the following statements. Tick whichever statement/s reflects how you feel. (Tick as many as apply.)

1 When it comes to key result areas
   A I know what is expected of me. ☐
   B I know how my job fits into the organization. ☐
   C I know when I've done a good job. ☐
   D When facing conflicting priorities, I know what to do. ☐

Look at the following statements. Tick whichever statement most closely describes what you would do.

2 Normally, when faced with deciding between conflicting priorities, I
   A Do what my boss wants me to do, even if it is less important. ☐

B Do what the client/customer wants me
   to do, even if it is less important.   ☐
C Do what I want to do.   ☐
D Judge what to do from my job
   description concerning my key result areas.   ☐

Tick which of the following tasks you think is most important.

3 My most important task is
   A Attending meetings.   ☐
   B Dealing with paperwork.   ☐
   C Dealing with people.   ☐
   D Dealing with crises.   ☐

For questions 4-8, tick the option that most applies to you.

4 When choosing which tasks to do first in a working day I
   choose
   A Those tasks that are quick to do.   ☐
   B Those tasks that are easy to do.   ☐
   C Those tasks that are hard to do.   ☐
   D Those tasks that will take a long time to do. ☐

5 Do you have a 'to do' list?
   A Yes.   ☐
   B No.   ☐
   C Sometimes.   ☐

(If you chose B go straight to question 7.)

6 Do you use it?
   A Yes.   ☐
   B No.   ☐
   C Sometimes.   ☐

7   Do you plan your time?
    A   Yes.   ☐
    B   No.   ☐
    C   Sometimes.   ☐

8   Do you stick to your plan?
    A   Yes.   ☐
    B   No.   ☐
    C   Sometimes.   ☐

ASSESSMENT 3: TASKS

This assessment will help you establish how effective you are at managing and implementing systems that will support you in making the best use of your time.

For questions 1-4, tick the answer that most applies to you.

1   Do you have a pending tray that you use?
    A   Yes.   ☐
    B   No.   ☐

2   Do you use a 'bring forward' or 'tickler' system?
    A   Yes.   ☐
    B   No.   ☐

3   Do you use a diary (either paper or computer)?
    A   Yes.   ☐
    B   No.   ☐

4   Do you have separate diaries for work and home?
    A   Yes.   ☐
    B   No.   ☐

Do you write appointments in you diary? Look at the list below. Tick whether you would find each item sometimes, often or rarely written in your diary.

5

Item	Sometimes	Often	Rarely
Appointment to see your boss/colleague			
Internal work meeting			
Client meeting			
Social meeting			
Doctor/dentist appointments			
Appointments to do with family (eg children's teacher, mother's home help etc)			
Jobs that need to be done (work)			
Jobs that need to be done (home)			
Notes to yourself			

Give yourself 1 POINT for each tick you have placed in the 'often' column.

SCORE

For the following two questions, tick the answer that most applies to you.

6   Do you have a filing system that you find easy to use?
   A   Yes. ☐
   B   No. ☐

7   Is your filing currently up to date?
   A   Yes. ☐
   B   No. ☐

Look at the following table. Tick the appropriate boxes.

8   How often do you use the following?

Item	Hourly	Daily	Weekly	Never
E-mail				
Voice mail				
Telephone				
Fax				
Postal service				
Face-to-face communication				

Look at the following questions. Again, tick which option applies most to you.

9   When you have material that needs to be read, but probably doesn't need any action, what do you do?
    A   Put it in a reading pile until you get round to it. ☐
    B   Plan time to read it. ☐
    C   Skim contents first, then either bin it or put it aside for later. ☐
    D   Carry it with you to read at a spare moment. ☐

10 How would you describe your desk?
    A   A complete mess but you know where everything is. ☐
    B   Quite tidy but with a lot of paper on it. ☐
    C   Very tidy – you clear it every day. ☐
    D   A complete mess and you can never find anything. ☐

11 How many trays are there on your desk?
    A   None. ☐
    B   One/two. ☐
    C   Three. ☐
    D   Four or more. ☐

12 When your post arrives, when do you look at it?
    A   Immediately. ☐
    B   The same day. ☐
    C   The same week. ☐
    D   When you get round to it. ☐

13 When dealing with e-mails what do you do?
- A Deal with them once a day at a specified time. ☐
- B Deal with them more than once a day. ☐
- C Read and respond to them as soon as
     they arrive. ☐
- D Leave them until you have time. ☐

14 In organizing outstanding papers related to your work
what do you do?
- A Put them in a pending tray. ☐
- B Leave them on your desk. ☐
- C Put them in a 'bring forward'/'tickler' system. ☐
- D Put them in your briefcase to take home. ☐

15 When do you check your voice mail?
- A Immediately. ☐
- B The same day. ☐
- C The same week. ☐
- D When you get round to it. ☐
- E You don't have voice mail. ☐

16 With paper are you more likely to
- A Throw it away as soon as you can? ☐
- B Hang on to it for a bit then throw it away? ☐
- C Hoard it for ages on the off-chance that
     you might need it? ☐

17 What papers are on your desk?
- A Only what you are currently working on. ☐
- B Plenty, all your ongoing tasks plus in-tray
     content and filing. ☐

18 Do you have a written 'to do' list?
- A Yes. ☐
- B No. ☐
- C Sometimes. ☐

19 How many items are on your 'to do' list?

    A   1-8   ☐

    B   9-15   ☐

    C   16+   ☐

20 On average, how much time during your working week do you spend doing tasks that you had planned for?

    A   Don't know.   ☐

    B   Not enough.   ☐

    C   Just the right amount of time.   ☐

21 Do you use the file management facilities on your PC?

    A   Yes.   ☐

    B   No.   ☐

    C   Sometimes.   ☐

Ideally, you should work through all 8 assessments to get an overall view of your time management 'fitness'. If, however, you wish to focus on your ability to manage your work ➡ Managing your work Fitness Profile p.27.

Managing people

People are time-consuming! Whether in a formal meeting or chatting around the water cooler, how you deal with people affects how well you do your job – and how time effectively. The following three assessments focus on managing people.

ASSESSMENT 4: PEOPLE

Look at the following questions. Tick your most likely response.

1 How well do you know people in other departments?

    A   Very well, I see them quite often.   ☐

    B   Not well, we speak on the phone occasionally.   ☐

    C   Not at all well. I have no reason to.   ☐

TRAINER'S WARNING

Don't forget to answer these questions honestly; make sure you get a true picture of your fitness!

2   What is your view about social chit chat at work?

A   It's a waste of time and I keep well out of it.   ☐

B   It's inevitable, but I try not to do too much of it.   ☐

C   It's important because you make friends that way.   ☐

D   I love it! It makes the day less dull.   ☐

3   How often do you help others out with their work?

A   Often – I like to help people if I can.   ☐

B   Sometimes, especially if I like them.   ☐

C   Rarely, people should do their own jobs properly.   ☐

TRAINER'S TIP

Feel free to change the genders or personnel in any of the examples offered; you may find this helps you relate to the situations.

4   How would you deal with someone who constantly misses deadlines you have set?

A   I make sure they know that it's not acceptable.   ☐

B   I don't give them any more important tasks.   ☐

C   I give them false deadlines.   ☐

D   I find out why they keep missing them.   ☐

5   What is the first thing that you do when faced with a mistake?

A   Find out who caused the mistake.   ☐

B   Find out what caused the mistake.   ☐

C   Fix the mistake.   ☐

6   If a colleague appears to be in a bad mood what do you do?

A   Ignore it, they'll get over it.   ☐

B   Try to find out what's wrong.   ☐
C   I think people should control their emotions,
     especially at work.   ☐

7   If a colleague has annoyed you what would you do?
    A   Speak to them about it.   ☐
    B   Forget about it.   ☐
    C   Let off steam to other colleagues.   ☐

8   How often do you ask for help or advice from a
    colleague?
    A   Fairly often.   ☐
    B   Sometimes.   ☐
    C   Rarely.   ☐

ASSESSMENT 5: MEETINGS

For many of us, work involves attending meetings. Some of
these meetings we find useful, yet more often we wonder
why we are there and what the meeting is supposed to
achieve. This assessment will help you establish where you
are weak and strong at dealing with meetings.

Look at the following questions. Tick the appropriate response.

1   How many meetings do you attend (either formal,
    informal or *ad hoc*)?
    A   2-5 per week.   ☐
    B   5-6 per month.   ☐
    C   None.   ☐
    D   More than 6 per week.   ☐

2   Do you prepare for meetings before you attend them
    by reading the agenda and supporting paperwork, or
    finding out what the meeting is about if it is *ad hoc*?
    A   Always.   ☐
    B   Sometimes.   ☐
    C   Rarely.   ☐

3 How confident do you feel about expressing your views in meetings?

   A Not very confident. ☐

   B Reasonably confident if I know the subject. ☐

   C Very confident, regardless of subject. ☐

4 Are you always clear about actions arising from meetings?

   A Yes – deadlines and actions are always agreed. ☐

   B Sometimes, usually I am clear about my own actions. ☐

   C Rarely, sometimes I'm not even sure why the meeting was being held. ☐

5 Are you always clear about the purpose of the meeting?

   A Sometimes. ☐

   B Usually. ☐

   C Rarely. ☐

6 If you find yourself in a meeting that you consider to be a waste of time do you

   A Stay? ☐

   B Leave? ☐

7 If you can see that people are getting off track during a meeting do you

   A Leave it to the Chair to sort out? ☐

   B Point it out? ☐

   C Ignore it? ☐

8 Do you take your own notes at meetings?

   A Yes, usually. ☐

   B Rarely, I normally wait for the minutes. ☐

9   How often do you complete all the actions you have been given at a meeting?
   A   Always.   ☐
   B   Usually.   ☐
   C   Rarely.   ☐

ASSESSMENT 6: INTERRUPTIONS

Interruptions are an inevitable part of life. If not handled effectively they can disrupt the best laid time management plans.

This assessment will help you establish what kinds of interruptions you are subject to; how many of them are of your own making and how many are caused by others.

Look at the following questions. Tick your most likely/the most appropriate response.

1   If you are interrupted in your work by a colleague, do you
   A   Drop everything to deal with them immediately?   ☐
   B   Tell them to come back later?   ☐

2   What is your view about being available to people?
   A   I think you should always be available to other people.   ☐
   B   I think you should only be 100% available to your boss.   ☐
   C   I think that you should have some time when you are not available to anyone.   ☐

3   How often do you play 'telephone tag' (ie you call and leave a message, they return your call and leave a message, you call back etc)?
   A   Daily.   ☐
   B   A couple of times a week.   ☐
   C   Rarely.   ☐

4 How do you view interruptions?
   A A part of life's rich tapestry. ☐
   B A pain – people shouldn't need to interrupt. ☐

5 At work, how often do you get uninterrupted time to yourself?
   A Several times a week. ☐
   B Several times a month. ☐
   C Hardly ever. ☐

6 How much of your time is spent fire fighting?
   A 0-30% ☐
   B 31-70% ☐
   C 71%+ ☐

7 By which of the following are you most likely to be interrupted? (*Tick as many as apply, then mark the number of boxes you ticked below.*)
   A A colleague has a problem that only you can solve. ☐
   B A client/customer has a problem that only you can solve. ☐
   C A colleague/boss giving you work or a message. ☐
   D Someone chasing you for something. ☐
   E You interrupt yourself because you remember something you haven't done. ☐

Number of boxes ticked   SCORE

Ideally, you should work through all 8 assessments to get an overall view of your skills fitness. If, however, you wish to focus on your ability to manage people ➡ Managing people Fitness Profile p.40.

Getting a life

Managing time is not just about prioritizing tasks or running tight meetings. It is not just about work! You also need to manage time outside of work, making sure you have time for your family, your friends and yourself. The following two assessments focus on getting a life.

TRAINER'S TIP

Feel free to change the genders in any of the examples offered; this may help you relate better to the situations.

TRAINER'S WARNING

Remember to answer these questions honestly – make sure you get a true picture of your fitness.

ASSESSMENT 7: BALANCING LIFE

A healthy, self-determined balance between life and work is crucial to effectiveness – including your ability to manage time. This assessment will help you analyze your current work-life balance and where you may need to make some changes or improvements.

For this assessment:

Never = I never do or think this
Sometimes = I sometimes do or think this
Often = I often do or think this

Look at the list of statements below. Circle the response ('Never', 'Sometimes', Often') which most applies to you.

1 I believe that people should keep work and separate home.

  Never   Sometimes   Often

2 When faced with a choice between pleasing my boss and pleasing my partner, I please my boss.

  Never   Sometimes   Often

3 I spend more time working than I do with my family.

   Never   Sometimes   Often

4 I find being at home restful.

   Never   Sometimes   Often

5 I feel satisfied with the balance I have between work
   and home life.

   Never   Sometimes   Often

6 I feel I have a healthy social life.

   Never   Sometimes   Often

7 My personal affairs (finances etc) are well organized.

   Never   Sometimes   Often

8 My house/home is just as I want it to be.

   Never   Sometimes   Often

9 On the whole, I feel I am achieving all I want to in my
   life.

   Never   Sometimes   Often

10 I stay late at work because it's expected of me.

   Never   Sometimes   Often

ASSESSMENT 8: MANAGING STRESS

Stress is part and parcel of life – at both work and home – and the ability to manage, and even use, it effectively is key to achieving whole life balance, and being more effective at work. This assessment will help you identify in what areas of your life you are currently suffering stress.

Look at the following questions (Tick as many options as apply, then mark the number of boxes you ticked below.)

1   Which of the following have you experienced over the last few months?

Being easily irritated ☐

Having difficulty concentrating for any length of time/ making simple decisions ☐

The quality of your sleep has deteriorated. Difficulty getting to sleep and/or waking during the night ☐

Feeling tired even when you wake up in the morning ☐

Losing your temper frequently ☐

Feeling generally run down and unwell ☐

Life seeming to be quite hopeless. Nothing seeming worthwhile and feeling really low ☐

Altered eating pattern. Loss of appetite or eating more food to comfort yourself ☐

Frequent headaches or indigestion ☐

Difficulty recalling information when required to do so ☐

Drinking more alcohol/smoking more cigarettes ☐

Experiencing dramatic mood swings ☐

Missing or being late for one or two important appointments ☐

Feeling unable to achieve your normal level of creativity ☐

Feeling inadequate and unable to cope ☐

Taking time off work ☐

Being panicked by the smallest thing ☐

Frequently repeating yourself in conversations ☐

Number of boxes ticked   SCORE

For questions 2-10, tick the most appropriate response.

2 How much time do you have just for yourself?
A About an hour a day. ☐
B A few hours a week. ☐
C A few hours a month. ☐
D Very little time ever. ☐

3 How often do you take proper exercise?
A At least 3 times a week. ☐
B Occasionally. ☐
C Rarely. ☐

4 Are you generally happy in your job?
A Yes. ☐
B No. ☐
C Sometimes. ☐

5 Do you have a good working relationship with your manager?
A No – you can't stand him/her. ☐
B Yes – you get on very well. ☐
C It's fine, but purely restricted to professional matters. ☐

6 When you are feeling under stress at work, which of the following do you do?
A Tell a friend. ☐
B Tell someone at home. ☐
C Keep it to yourself. ☐
D Tell someone at work. ☐

7 Are you coping financially?
A Yes. ☐
B No. ☐

8 When faced with a stressful situation do you
A Accept it? ☐
B Ignore it and hope it will go away? ☐
C Tackle the problem? ☐

9   How easy do you find it to express your personal
        feelings and thoughts?
   A   Very easy – you can talk to anyone.   ☐
   B   Easy at home – can't do it at work.   ☐
   C   Easy at work – can't do it at home.   ☐
   D   Not at all easy – you tend to keep things
       bottled up.   ☐

10 Do you have any hobbies or interests?
   A   Yes.   ☐
   B   No.   ☐

Ideally, you will now have completed all 8 assessments and
tested your overall skills fitness. If so ➡ Fitness Profile p.23.

   If, however, you have chosen to focus on getting a life ➡
Getting a life Fitness Profile p.50.

Fitness Profile

Well done, you've gone through Fitness Assessment – now you can find out the results!

Fitness Profile allows you to evaluate your current skills fitness – your strengths, weaknesses and priorities for action. It builds up into a fitness profile unique to you.

Fitness profiles 1-3 relate directly to assessments 1-3. Similarly, profiles 4-6 and 7-8.

Managing your work

The following three profiles will help you build up a picture of how well you manage time when managing your work.

PROFILE 1: ATTITUDE

Having a positive attitude about your own abilities, the amount you have to do and the support available is half the battle towards effective time management. So how did you do? Look back to p.5-6 in Fitness Assessment; remind yourself of the questionnaire – and your responses. Make a note of your responses below, eg if you answered B for question 1 tick the box in the B column opposite Question 1.

	A	**B**	**C**
Question 1	☐	☐	☐
Question 2	☐	☐	☐
Question 3	☐	☐	☐
Question 4	☐	☐	☐
Question 5	☐	☐	☐

Now check out whether your answers to these questions mean you have a healthy attitude towards managing your time at work.

QUESTION 1
When thinking about managing my time
   A   I always feel completely out of
       control ➡   **0 POINTS**
   B   I occasionally feel in control ➡   **3 POINTS**
   C   I usually feel in control ➡   **5 POINTS**

SCORE

QUESTION 2
When thinking about my work
   A   I don't much care what happens ➡ **0 POINTS**

B   I care so much I get stressed ➡ **1 POINT**
C   I feel excited and interested ➡ **5 POINTS**

SCORE

QUESTION 3

I believe that work is

   A   Key to feeling worthwhile ➡ **5 POINTS**
   B   A means of getting money ➡ **3 POINTS**
   C   An interruption to real life ➡ **0 POINTS**

SCORE

QUESTION 4

When I have too much to do

   A   I see it as a challenge ➡ **5 POINTS**
   B   I get angry and frustrated ➡ **0 POINTS**
   C   I become less able to deliver ➡ **3 POINTS**

SCORE

QUESTION 5

I think that

   A   Every task should be completed to the highest quality ➡ **0 POINTS**
   B   Every task should be completed to a minimum standard ➡ **3 POINTS**
   C   Some tasks should be completed to high quality and some not done at all ➡ **5 POINTS**

SCORE

If you chose **C** well done, some jobs don't need to be done at all. If you chose A you are probably often behind tasks. Now add up your scores

TOTAL ASSESSMENT 1 SCORE

For assessment 1, the higher you score the more positive your attitude, and the better able you are to manage your work. Your **maximum** score is **25**.
Your **minimum** score is **0**.

PROFILE 2: PRIORITIES

To prioritize effectively you need to have a clear understanding about who and what is important. Look back to p.6 in Fitness Assessment and remind yourself of the questions and the options you ticked. Make a note of the options (A-D) you ticked below, eg if you chose C for question 4 tick the box in the C column opposite Question 4.

	A	B	C	D
Question 1	☐	☐	☐	☐
Question 2	☐	☐	☐	☐
Question 3	☐	☐	☐	☐
Question 4	☐	☐	☐	☐
Question 5	☐	☐	☐	☐
Question 6	☐	☐	☐	☐
Question 7	☐	☐	☐	☐
Question 8	☐	☐	☐	☐

Now check out whether your answers to these questions mean you know how to prioritize effectively.

QUESTION 1
When it comes to key result areas
A   I know what is expected of me ➡ **3 POINTS**
B   I know how my job fits into the organization ➡ **3 POINTS**
C   I know when I've done a good job ➡ **3 POINTS**
D   When facing conflicting priorities, I know what to do. ➡ **3 POINTS**

SCORE

If you are clear about your job, how it fits in and what is expected of you, then you will be more effective.

QUESTION 2

Normally, when faced with deciding between conflicting priorities, I

    A Do what my boss wants me to do, even if it is less important ➡ **1 POINT**

    B Do what the client/customer wants me to do, even if it less important ➡ **5 POINTS**

    C Do what I want to do ➡ **1 POINT**

    D Judge what to do from my job description concerning my key result areas ➡ **3 POINTS**

SCORE

If you chose **B** well done – you realize that the client or customer is the priority. If you chose A, you need to consider if you are simply trying to please.

QUESTION 3

My most important task is?

    A Attending meetings ➡ **1 POINT**

    B Dealing with paperwork ➡ **1 POINT**

    C Dealing with people ➡ **5 POINTS**

    D Dealing with crises ➡ **3 POINTS**

SCORE

If you chose **C** you realize that nearly everything we do at work is for people. If you chose D, yes, crises do have to be dealt with. But remember, self-inflicted crises should occur infrequently.

QUESTION 4

When choosing which tasks to do first in a working day I choose

    A Those tasks that are quick to do ➡ **1 POINT**

    B Those tasks that are easy to do ➡ **1 POINT**

    C Those tasks that are hard to do ➡ **5 POINTS**

    D Those tasks that will take a long time to do ➡ **3 POINTS**

SCORE

Well done if you chose **C**. Doing hard tasks first helps with task management. If you chose A, remember that 'quick' tasks should be done in spare moments.

QUESTION 5
Do you have a 'to do' list?

A	Yes	➡	5 POINTS
B	No	➡	0 POINTS
C	Sometimes	➡	3 POINTS

SCORE

A is the preferred answer. If you chose B you may forget to do tasks and get interrupted often.

QUESTION 6
Do you use it?

A	Yes	➡	5 POINTS
B	No	➡	0 POINTS
C	Sometimes	➡	1 POINT

SCORE

Clearly, you need to use it!

QUESTION 7
Do you plan your time?

A	Yes	➡	5 POINTS
B	No	➡	0 POINTS
C	Sometimes	➡	1 POINT

SCORE

A is the preferred answer. If you chose B you may be gaining a reputation for being unreliable.

QUESTION 8

Do you stick to your plan?

    A   Yes   →   **5 POINTS**

    B   No   →   **0 POINTS**

    C   Sometimes   →   **3 POINTS**

SCORE

If you chose **A** then great. If you chose C that is probably realistic – we need to be flexible to be time effective.

Now add up your scores

TOTAL ASSESSMENT 2 SCORE

> For assessment 2, the higher you score the better able you are to identify, and see through, priorities.
> Your **maximum** score is **47**.
> Your **minimum** score is **3**.

PROFILE 3: TASKS

Your ability to manage tasks is highly dependent upon your ability to use simple, effective systems that will ease the flow of work across your desk. Additionally, your ability to discipline yourself to stick to some key routines and make yourself do tasks that you find irritating or boring, such as filing, will help you manage time effectively.

Look back to p.8 in Fitness Assessment and remind yourself of questions 1-4 and your responses. Make a note of your responses below, eg if you chose A for question 2 tick the box in the A column opposite Question 2. Remember, for this question A = Yes, B = No.

	A	**B**
Question 1	☐	☐
Question 2	☐	☐
Question 3	☐	☐
Question 4	☐	☐

QUESTION 1
Do you have a pending tray that you use?

For question 1 the preferred response is **B** ➡ **3 POINTS**.
If you chose A, the tray holds paper you don't know what to do
with.   SCORE

QUESTION 2
Do you use a 'bring forward' or 'tickler' system?

Top marks if you chose **A** ➡   **3 POINTS**
          SCORE

QUESTION 3
Do you use a diary (either paper or computer)?

A diary is *crucial* to your ability to manage
time; **A** ➡   **3 POINTS**
          SCORE

QUESTION 4
Do you have separate diaries for work and home?

B is the preferred response ➡ **3 POINTS**. If you chose A, you
probably find yourself over-committing.
          SCORE

          TOTAL SCORE

QUESTION 5
Look back to p.9 in Fitness Assessment and make a note of
your score for question 5 here   ☐

QUESTION 6
Do you have a filing system that you find easy to use?
Look back to p.9 in Fitness Assessment; make a note of your
response (A or B) to question 6   ☐

Remember, for this question A = Yes, B = No.
If you answered **A** ➡ **3 POINTS**

SCORE

QUESTION 7
Is your filing currently up to date?

Look back to p. in Fitness Assessment; make a note of your
response to question 7   ☐
Remember, for this question A = Yes, B = No.
If you answered **A** ➡ **3 POINTS**

SCORE

QUESTION 8
Look back to p.10 in Fitness Assessment. Circle the options you
ticked on the table below. Each option has an individual score.

Item	Hourly	Daily	Weekly	Never
E-mail	1	5	3	0
Voice mail	1	5	3	0
Telephone	2	5	5	0
Fax	1	2	5	0
Postal service	0	3	5	1
Face-to-face communication	3	5	1	0

SCORE

Look back to p.10-12 in Fitness Assessment; remind yourself of
questions 9-21 and your responses. Note of your individual
responses below, eg if you chose B for question 9 write 'B' and
'plan time to read it' on the dotted line below Question 9.

QUESTION 9
When you have material that needs to be read, but probably
doesn't need any action, what do you do?

....

   A   Not likely to reduce your stress levels ➡ **0 POINTS**
   B   You still have that pile bothering you ➡ **3 POINTS**

C   You get rid of bits of paper that you are not going
     to do anything with. *(Ideally, you'd put it in a
     recycling bin. If you do that then give yourself
     10 points!)* ➡   **5 POINTS**

D   You are carting around paper that you may never
     read. ➡   **3 POINTS**

SCORE

QUESTION 10

How would you describe your desk?

....

A   You probably seem disorganized ➡ **3 POINTS**

B   People are reluctant to leave paper on your desk,
     which increases interruptions ➡   **3 POINTS**

C   Well done ➡   **5 POINTS**

D   People give you work in person. You experience a
     fair bit of stress ➡   **0 POINTS**

SCORE

QUESTION 11

How many trays are there on your desk?

....

A   This is a good answer, if you are filing paper
     away ➡   **3 POINTS**

B   You can locate documents fairly quickly. If you
     have two trays but they are stuffed and you
     don't know what's in them, deduct from
     your score ➡   **5 POINTS**

C   You must be hoarding paper that could be
     filed ➡   **3 POINTS**

D   The proper place for paperwork is first the bin
     (unless you can justify keeping it), secondly the 'bring
     forward' system and thirdly the filing
     system ➡   **0 POINTS**

SCORE

QUESTION 12

When your post arrives, when do you look at it?

....

A   Nowadays anything urgent is faxed, phoned or e-mailed ➡ **3 POINTS**

B   Provided you open it early enough to deal with anything urgent for the day, this is a healthy approach ➡ **5 POINTS**

C   You spend a lot of time fire fighting or finding out information too late to do anything with it ➡ **0 POINTS**

D   You are so overwhelmed that finding time is hard to do ➡ **0 POINTS**

SCORE

QUESTION 13

When dealing with e-mails what do you do?

....

A   Good ➡ **5 POINTS**

B   OK, if you are doing it systematically and not simply reacting ➡ **3 POINTS**

C   You don't take into account the time you spend on this ➡ **1 POINT**

D   This is not appropriate ➡ **0 POINTS**

SCORE

QUESTION 14

In organizing outstanding papers what do you do?

....

A   You are probably usually behind on your work, carry a fair amount of stress and get anxious about what is lurking in the pending tray ➡ **0 POINTS**

B   You suffer from the same symptoms as above ➡ **3 POINTS**

C   Excellent ➡ **5 POINTS**

D   You should very rarely have to take work
home   ➡   **3 POINTS**

SCORE

QUESTION 15
When do you check your voice mail?

A   Good   ➡   **5 POINTS**
B   It's OK to do this   ➡   **5 POINTS**
C   You are always running behind, turning up at the
wrong place at the wrong time and have a
reputation for never returning phone
calls   ➡   **0 POINTS**
D   You experience the same sorts of problems
as in C   ➡   **0 POINTS**
E   People are constantly ringing you about trivial
matters   ➡   **0 POINTS**

SCORE

QUESTION 16
With paper you are more likely to

A   Good   ➡   **5 POINTS**
B   You waste time seeing if it is clutter
which can be chucked   ➡   **3 POINTS**
C   Clutter is clogging up your ability to
be effective   ➡   **0 POINTS**

SCORE

QUESTION 17
What papers are on your desk?

A   Good   ➡   **5 POINTS**
B   You appear inefficient   ➡   **0 POINTS**

SCORE

QUESTION 18
Do you have a written 'to do' list?

....

    A Good ➡   **5 POINTS**

    B Disaster ➡   **0 POINTS**

    C Could do better! ➡   **1 POINT**

SCORE

QUESTION 19
How many items are on your 'to do' list?

....

    A Well done ➡   **5 POINTS**

    B You are unlikely to manage this ➡ **3 POINTS**

    C Quite unrealistic! ➡   **0 POINTS**

SCORE

QUESTION 20
On average, how much time during your working week do you spend doing tasks that you had planned for?

....

    A You are just reacting to tasks ➡ **0 POINTS**

    B You don't know where you need to
        improve ➡   **3 POINTS**

    C Great! ➡   **5 POINTS**

SCORE

QUESTION 21
Do you use the file management facilities on your PC?

....

    A Good ➡   **5 POINTS**

    B Your files are a mess ➡   **0 POINTS**

    C Room for improvement! ➡   **3 POINTS**

SCORE

Now add up your scores

TOTAL ASSESSMENT 3 SCORE

For assessment 3, the higher you score the more adept you are at managing and implementing systems to support your work.
Your **maximum** score is **127**.
Your **minimum** score is **0**.

So how fit are you at managing your work? Look back to p.28 for your score for assessment 1 and write it down here ☐
Now your assessment 2 score ☐
Now your assessment 3 score ☐

Add these individual scores together to make your **total managing your work score**:

TOTAL MANAGING YOUR WORK SCORE

The higher your total score the more able you are to manage your work – and your time.
Your **maximum** score is **199**.
Your **minimum** score is **3**.

 Congratulations, you are already fit at managing your work. There is always room for improvement, however!

 You are moderately fit. You can be positive and well organized, but you may be missing a few tricks. You could do with building your fitness.

 You are not skills fit! You need to take action to improve your ability to manage your work.

Ideally, you should work through all 8 assessments, profiles and work-outs to improve your overall fitness. However, if you have chosen to focus on developing your ability to manage your work ➡ Managing your work work-out p.67. Before doing this, however, it is a good idea to do some quick mental preparation ➡ Warm-up p.61.

Managing people

How you deal with people affects how well you do your job – and how time effectively. So how did you do?

PROFILE 4: PEOPLE

Look back to p.12-14 in Fitness Assessment; make a note of the options (A-D) you ticked below, eg if you chose C for question 5 tick the box in the C column opposite Question 5.

	A	B	C	D
Question 1	☐	☐	☐	☐
Question 2	☐	☐	☐	☐
Question 3	☐	☐	☐	☐
Question 4	☐	☐	☐	☐
Question 5	☐	☐	☐	☐
Question 6	☐	☐	☐	☐
Question 7	☐	☐	☐	☐
Question 8	☐	☐	☐	☐

Now check out whether your responses mean you know how to manage people well.

QUESTION 1

How well do you know people in other departments?

For question 1 the preferred response is **A**, 'Very well, I see them quite often.' You probably find that people are very co-operative and helpful   ➡   **3 POINTS**

SCORE

QUESTION 2
What is your view about social chit chat at work?

The preferred response is **C**, 'It's important because you make friends that way.' You will probably both give, and receive, help often ➡ **3 POINTS**

 SCORE

QUESTION 3
How often do you help others out with their work?

A, 'Often – I like to help people if I can', is the preferred response. However, be aware that helping others can interfere with your own work ➡ **3 POINTS**

SCORE

QUESTION 4
How would you deal with someone who constantly misses deadlines you have set?

For question 4 the preferred response is **D** – 'I find out why they keep missing them' ➡ **3 POINTS**
If you chose C (give them false deadlines) you are not getting to the root of the problem and may still have to chase persistent offenders.

SCORE

QUESTION 5
What is the first thing that you do when faced with a mistake?

The preferred answer is **B** – 'Find out what caused the mistake.' You generally get to the bottom of what caused the mistake (though rarely who) and can usually prevent it happening again ➡ **3 POINTS**
If you chose C (fix it) you'll find yourself dealing with the same mistakes again.

SCORE

QUESTION 6

If a colleague appears to be in a bad mood what do you do?

The preferred response is **B** – 'Try to find out what's wrong.' This takes time, but you can often say something useful ➡ **3 POINTS**. If you chose C ('I think people should control their emotions') you probably don't get as much support and sympathy as you need.

SCORE

QUESTION 7

If a colleague has annoyed you what would you do?

A, 'Speak to them about it', is the preferred response. It tends to save you time in the long run ➡ **3 POINTS** Forgetting about it (B) is not an option; the same colleague will do the same thing again.

SCORE

QUESTION 8

How often do you ask for help or advice from a colleague?

The preferred answer is **A**, 'Fairly often.' Others can spot different ways of doing things ➡ **3 POINTS**

SCORE

Now add up your scores

TOTAL ASSESSMENT 4 SCORE

For assessment 4, the higher you score the better able you are to get on with, and deal with, people.
Your **maximum** score is **24**.
Your **minimum** score is **0**.

PROFILE 5: MEETINGS

Look back to p.14-16 in Fitness Assessment and remind yourself of the questions and your responses. Make a note of the options (A-D) you ticked below, eg if you chose A for question 2 tick the box in the A column opposite Question 2.

	A	B	C	D
Question 1	☐	☐	☐	☐
Question 2	☐	☐	☐	☐
Question 3	☐	☐	☐	☐
Question 4	☐	☐	☐	☐
Question 5	☐	☐	☐	☐
Question 6	☐	☐	☐	☐
Question 7	☐	☐	☐	☐
Question 8	☐	☐	☐	☐
Question 9	☐	☐	☐	☐

Now check out whether your answers to these questions mean you get the most out of meetings.

QUESTION 1
How many meetings do you attend (either formal, informal or *ad hoc*?)

A	2-5 per week ➡	**3 POINTS**
B	5-6 per month ➡	**1 POINT**
C	None ➡	**0 POINTS**
D	More than 6 per week ➡	**0 POINTS**

SCORE

Well done if you chose **A**. You need to meet people to find out what's going on and pass on, or receive, information. If you chose D you probably spend so much time in meetings you don't have time to do the actions.

QUESTION 2

Do you prepare for meetings before you attend them by reading the agenda and supporting paperwork, or finding out what the meeting is about if it is *ad hoc*?

A　Always　➡️　　　　　　　**3 POINTS**
B　Sometimes　➡️　　　　　**1 POINT**
C　Rarely　➡️　　　　　　　**0 POINTS**

SCORE

If you chose **A** well done. If you chose C you probably often wonder why on earth you are at the meeting.

QUESTION 3

How confident do you feel about expressing your views in meetings?

A　Not very confident　➡️　　**0 POINTS**
B　Reasonably confident, if I know
　　the subject　➡️　　　　　**1 POINT**
C　Very confident, regardless of
　　subject　➡️　　　　　　　**3 POINTS**

SCORE

If you chose **C** you probably find meetings productive and useful. If you don't know a subject you will sometimes ask a question which highlights an issue or makes other people see the situation differently. If you chose B then well done too.

QUESTION 4

Are you always clear about actions arising from meetings?

A　Yes – deadlines and actions are
　　always agreed　➡️　　　　**3 POINTS**
B　Sometimes, usually I am clear about my
　　own actions　➡️　　　　　**1 POINT**
C　Rarely, sometimes I'm not even sure why
　　the meeting was being held　➡️　**0 POINTS**

SCORE

If you chose **A**, great.

QUESTION 5

Are you always clear about the purpose of the meeting?

A   Sometimes ➡   **1 POINT**

B   Usually ➡   **3 POINTS**

C   Rarely ➡   **0 POINTS**

SCORE

If you chose **B** well done. You seldom end up at meetings where you are not clear what it's about and why you are there. If you chose C you tend to see meetings as a waste of time.

QUESTION 6

If you find yourself in a meeting that you consider to be a waste of time do you

A   Stay? ➡   **1 POINT**

B   Leave? ➡   **3 POINTS**

SCORE

If you manage to leave a meeting without causing offence to those remaining then well done! If staying means maintaining a relationship then it's not such a bad thing.

QUESTION 7

If you can see that people are getting off track during a meeting do you

A   Leave it to the Chair to sort out? ➡   **0 POINTS**

B   Point it out? ➡   **3 POINTS**

C   Ignore it? ➡   **0 POINTS**

SCORE

It is important to make it clear when people are straying, but be careful not to offend people. You can't afford to ignore the problem or leave it to the Chair – maybe the Chair won't spot the problem; maybe the Chair is the problem!

QUESTION 8

Do you take your own notes at meetings?

- A   Yes, usually ➡   **3 POINTS**
- B   Rarely, I normally wait for
      the minutes ➡   **0 POINTS**

SCORE

If you chose **A** you get through actions more quickly and remember more accurately what occurred. If you wait for the minutes (B) they often arrive late and you are suddenly reminded of a key action or deadline.

QUESTION 9

How often do you complete all the actions you have been given at a meeting?

- A   Always ➡   **3 POINTS**
- B   Usually ➡   **3 POINTS**
- C   Rarely ➡   **3 POINTS**

SCORE

If you chose **B** you recognize that sometimes actions turn out to be unnecessary, or someone else could do them earlier/better.

Now add up your scores

TOTAL ASSESSMENT 5 SCORE

For assessment 5, the higher you score the greater your ability to get the most out of meetings.
Your **maximum** score is **27**.
Your **minimum** score is **1**.

PROFILE 6: INTERRUPTIONS

Look back to p.16-17 in Fitness Assessment; remind yourself of questions 1-6 and your responses. Make a note of your individual responses, and what they mean, below. For example, if you chose option B for question 1 write 'B' and 'Tell them to come back later' on the dotted below Question 1.

QUESTION 1

If you are interrupted in your work by a colleague what do you do?

....

For question 1 the preferred answer is B, tell them (politely) to come back later ➡ **3 POINTS**

If you deal with them immediately, regardless of urgency (A), you are not making good use of time. SCORE

QUESTION 2

What is your view about being available to people?

....

'I think that you should have some time when you are not available to anyone' (C) is the preferred response. This may sound extreme, but you will find it easier to meet deadlines and have time to be supportive to colleagues ➡ **3 POINTS**

SCORE

QUESTION 3

How often do you play 'telephone tag'?

If you chose C, 'Rarely', then great! Telephone tag is a frustrating, and time-wasting, activity ➡ **3 POINTS**

SCORE

QUESTION 4

How do you view interruptions?

As 'part of life's rich tapestry' (A) is a positive, and realistic, attitude ➡ **3 POINTS**

SCORE

QUESTION 5

At work, how often do you get uninterrupted time?

....

The preferred answer is 'several times a week' – **A**. It may take an act of will, but getting time to yourself is vital ➡ **3 POINTS**

SCORE

QUESTION 6

How much of your time is spent fire fighting?

Well done if you chose **A** – 0-30% ➡ **3 POINTS**

If you chose B or C, ask yourself whether the fire fighting is a result of your mistakes or due to organizational inadequacies.

SCORE

QUESTION 7

Look back to p.17 in Fitness Assessment and write down the total number of boxes you ticked here ☐

For each tick ➡ **–3 POINTS**

SCORE

For this question, the more boxes you ticked the less effective you are at handling interruptions.

Now add up your scores, deducting any points scored for question 7

TOTAL ASSESSMENT 6 SCORE

For assessment 6, the higher you score the more adept you are at handling interruptions.

Your **maximum** score is **18**.

Your **minimum** score is **–15**.

So how fit are you at managing people? Look back to p.42 for your score for assessment 4 and write it down here ☐
Now your assessment 5 score ☐
Now your assessment 6 score ☐

Add these individual scores together to make your **total managing people score**:

TOTAL MANAGING PEOPLE SCORE

The higher your total score the more confident, and able, you are to manage people, and the greater your ability to manage time.
Your **maximum** score is **69**.
Your **minimum** score is **–14**.

 43–69 Congratulations, you already have a healthy approach to managing people and are skills fit. There is always room for improvement, however!

 15–42 You are moderately fit. You can manage people well at times but there are situations that you find difficult. You could do with building your fitness.

 –4–14 You are not skills fit! You need to do some work on improving your ability to manage people.

Ideally, you should work through all 8 assessments, profiles and work-outs to improve your overall fitness. However, if you have chosen to focus on developing your ability to manage people ➡ Managing people work-out p.84. Before doing this, however, it is a good idea to do some quick mental preparation ➡ Warm-up p.61.

Getting a life

Managing your time so that you have both a work and a home life is crucial to your overall effectiveness – and well-being. The following two profiles will help you assess your current work-life balance, and identify causes of stress.

PROFILE 7: BALANCING LIFE

Look back to p.18-19 in Fitness Assessment; remind yourself of the statements and the options you chose. For each statement circle the option ('Never', 'Sometimes', Often') you chose below. Each option has a related score.

STATEMENT 1
I believe that people should keep work and home separate.

Never	Sometimes	Often	Score
5	3	0	☐

One is bound to intrude on the other.

STATEMENT 2
When faced with a choice between pleasing my boss and pleasing my partner, I please my boss.

Never	Sometimes	Often	Score
3	5	0	☐

If you go for either extreme, you are in trouble somewhere.

STATEMENT 3
I spend more time working than I do with my family.

Never	Sometimes	Often	Score
5	3	0	☐

Spending more time working than with the family is a fairly common experience, especially for men. However, the issue is not how much time you spend, but when you do spend time with your family, that they think of it as focused on them.

STATEMENT 4

I find being at home restful.

Never	**Sometimes**	**Often**	**Score**
0	3	5	☐

This is actually quite an important issue, to which I hope you responded honestly. The important thing to note here is not to judge yourself negatively if there are times when you do feel like you're 'escaping' to work!

STATEMENT 5

I feel satisfied with the balance I have between work and home life.

Never	**Sometimes**	**Often**	**Score**
0	3	5	☐

This is important. If you feel satisfied with the balance, there is a fairly good chance that you are operating effectively in both areas.

STATEMENT 6

I feel I have a healthy social life.

Never	**Sometimes**	**Often**	**Score**
0	3	5	☐

Our minds need variety and difference in order to feel stimulated and work well. Thus it is important to spend time socially with other people, especially friends, in addition to the time you spend with your family or work colleagues.

STATEMENT 7

My personal affairs (finances etc) are well organized.

Never	**Sometimes**	**Often**	**Score**
0	3	5	☐

Many people can live in a state of financial confusion, living from one overdraft to the next and loving to use credit cards because it doesn't feel like real money! Money of course is not the most important thing, but it becomes important when you don't have it.

STATEMENT 8
My house/home is just as I want it to be.

Never	Sometimes	Often	Score
0	3	5	☐

Again, this is fairly important. If you are dissatisfied with your living circumstances, that's bound to have an effect on how you feel about yourself in all other contexts.

STATEMENT 9
On the whole, I feel I am achieving all I want to in my life.

Never	Sometimes	Often	Score
0	3	5	☐

This all depends on how big your ambitions are, of course, but it is important for your sense of self-worth to feel that at least you are on the right track.

STATEMENT 10
I stay late at work because it's expected of me.

Never	Sometimes	Often	Score
0	5	0	☐

Obviously, for everyone there are times when you need to stay late at work. However, if you consistently have to stay late because you can't get through the work then something is wrong with either the job or the way you are managing your time.

Now add up your scores

TOTAL ASSESSMENT 7 SCORE

For assessment 7, the higher you score the better your ability to balance your life.
Your **maximum** score is **50**.
Your **minimum** score is **0**.

PROFILE 8: MANAGING STRESS

QUESTION 1

Look back to p.20 in Fitness Assessment. Make a note of
the total number of boxes you ticked here ☐
For each tick ➡ **–1 POINT**

SCORE

For this question, the more boxes you ticked the less effective
you are at managing stress.

For this question, the **minimum** score is **–18**, the
maximum score is **0**.

Your optimal score is any score between 0 and –6.

The closer your score to –18, the more likely it is you are
suffering from unhealthy stress.

If your score is –7 to –12 you are close to being over-
stressed, depending on how close your score is to –12.
You need to address this now, so complete the work-
out and stick at it.

If you have a score between –12 and –18 you are
suffering an unhealthy amount of stress. If you ticked
the box saying that life seems quite worthless and
nothing seems worthwhile then you have a serious
problem. I strongly suggest that if your score is between
–12 and –18 you need to go and see your doctor and
talk through some of what is affecting you. Don't think
that you can sort this out by yourself without help.
Without wishing to make you feel anxious, if you don't
seek help it may get worse.

For the remaining questions, look back to p.21-22 in Fitness
Assessment, remind yourself of the questions and your
responses. Make a note of the options you ticked overleaf.

	A	**B**	**C**	**D**
Question 2	☐	☐	☐	☐
Question 3	☐	☐	☐	☐
Question 4	☐	☐	☐	☐
Question 5	☐	☐	☐	☐
Question 6	☐	☐	☐	☐
Question 7	☐	☐	☐	☐
Question 8	☐	☐	☐	☐
Question 9	☐	☐	☐	☐
Question 10	☐	☐	☐	☐

QUESTION 2

How much time do you have just for yourself?

A About an hour a day ➡   **5 POINTS**
B A few hours a week ➡   **3 POINTS**
C A few hours a month ➡   **1 POINT**
D Very little time ever ➡   **0 POINTS**

SCORE

Well done if you chose **A**; this really is very good. If you chose D, you definitely need to do something about this.

QUESTION 3

How often do you take proper exercise?

A At least 3 times a week ➡   **5 POINTS**
B Occasionally ➡   **3 POINTS**
C Rarely ➡   **0 POINTS**

SCORE

Again, **A** is the preferred answer. When you exercise regularly you find it much easier to deal with stressful situations.

QUESTION 4

Are you generally happy in your job?

A Yes ➡   **5 POINTS**

B No ➡ **0 POINTS**
C Sometimes ➡ **3 POINTS**

SCORE

Of course, **A** is the preferred answer.

QUESTION 5
Do you have a good working relationship with your manager?
   A No – you can't stand him/her ➡ **0 POINTS**
   B Yes – you get on very well ➡ **5 POINTS**
   C It's fine, but purely restricted to professional
      matters ➡ **3 POINTS**

SCORE

If you chose **B** well done. Being able to express your feelings openly to your manager is key; a poor relationship with the boss is often cited as a major cause of stress. If you chose C, remember that you don't have to be best friends, but it does help to share the burden when you are feeling stressed.

QUESTION 6
When you are feeling under stress at work, which of the following do you do?
   A Tell a friend ➡ **3 POINTS**
   B Tell someone at home ➡ **3 POINTS**
   C Keep it to yourself ➡ **0 POINTS**
   D Tell someone at work ➡ **5 POINTS**

SCORE

D is the preferred answer. A colleague is best placed to offer advice and relevant practical support.

QUESTION 7
Are you coping financially?
   A Yes ➡ **5 POINTS**
   B No ➡ **0 POINTS**

SCORE

Feeling under financial pressure can significantly affect your effectiveness. You may need some financial advice if you chose B.

QUESTION 8

When faced with a stressful situation do you

A   Accept it?   **5 POINTS**

B   Ignore it and hope it will go away? ➡ **0 POINTS**

C   Tackle the problem? ➡   **5 POINTS**

SCORE

C is the preferred response. However, A can sometimes be a good way of handling a problem that is causing you stress.

QUESTION 9

How easy do you find it to express your personal feelings and thoughts?

A   Very easy – you can talk to anyone ➡**5 POINTS**

B   Easy at home – can't do it at work ➡ **3 POINTS**

C   Easy at work – can't do it at home ➡ **1 POINT**

D   Not at all easy – you tend to keep things bottled up   **0 POINTS**

SCORE

If you chose D, remember that there is a strong correlation between those who keep things bottled up and those who get stressed.

QUESTION 10

Do you have any hobbies or interests?

A   Yes ➡   **5 POINTS**

B   No ➡   **0 POINTS**

SCORE

Hobbies act as an active distraction and can be helpful when dealing with stress.

Now add up your scores, deducting any minus points scored for question 1

TOTAL ASSESSMENT 8 SCORE

For assessment 8, the higher you score the better able you are to handle, and minimize, stress.
Your **maximum** score is **45**.
Your **minimum** score is **–18**.

So how healthy are you at getting a life?
Look back to p.52 for your score for assessment 7 and write it down here ☐
Now your assessment 8 score ☐

Add these individual scores together to make your **getting a life score**:

TOTAL GETTING A LIFE SCORE

The higher your total score the more able you are to minimize stress and get a life.
Your **maximum** score is **95**.
Your **minimum** score is **–18**.

 Congratulations, you are fit at getting a life. There is always room for improvement, however!

 You are moderately fit. You could do with building your fitness.

 You are not skills fit. You need to do some work on building your ability to get a life.

Ideally, you should now have worked through all 8 assessments and profiles. If so, turn to the following page to discover your **overall time management fitness level**.

If, however, you have focused on developing your ability to get a life ➡ Getting a life work-out p.99. Before doing this, however, you need to do some quick mental preparation ➡ Warm-up p.6.

How good are you at time management?

Ideally, you should now have completed all 8 assessments and profiles, and have a good idea of how fit you are in time management.

Personal fitness profile

Look back at how you scored in the three sections:
  Managing your work
  Managing people, and
  Getting a life.

Make a note of your individual total scores for these sections below:

Managing your work ☐
Managing people ☐
Getting a life ☐
What is your total time management score?

TOTAL TIME MANAGEMENT SCORE

 233-363 Congratulations, you are fit at managing time. Are there any areas you could improve still further?

 102-232 You are moderately fit. You could do with building your fitness.

 -29-101 You are not skills fit! You need to do some work and build your time management skills.

Now take another look at your individual total scores for the three sections. Circle these scores overleaf.

	UNFIT	REASONABLY FIT	FIT
Managing your work	3-68	69-134	135-199
Managing people	-4-14	15-42	43-69
Getting a life	-18-20	21-58	59-95

Are you strong or weak in any particular section/skills area? Are you, for example, good at managing your time at work but bad at managing your time to get a life? Or perhaps you have strengths and weaknesses across all sections? Look back to your individual scores in profiles 1-8. Can you identify any particular strengths or weaknesses?

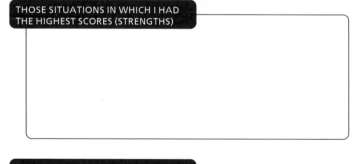

THOSE SITUATIONS IN WHICH I HAD THE HIGHEST SCORES (STRENGTHS)

THOSE SITUATIONS IN WHICH I HAD THE LOWEST SCORES (WEAKNESSES)

Congratulations on your strengths, but you do need to take action to develop your weaker areas.

Before moving on to Work-out, however, you need to do some quick mental preparation ➡ Warm-up opposite.

Warm-up

It is a good idea to do a quick mental warm-up before tackling the exercises in Work-out. Take a few moments to reflect on why you want to manage your time better. Now complete the following.

- What is the most important benefit to you of managing your time more effectively? ....
....
- Who else will benefit from you managing your time more effectively? ....
....
- Imagine how you feel on a day when you have completed everything that needed to be done on that day, and you go away when you had planned to; imagine what you are going to do that evening. Write it down ....
- Write down any mental blocks that might prevent you from achieving your goal ....
....

At the beginning of each day, take some time out to visualize what you want to have completed by the end of the day, including time spent with your family/friends.

You are now ready to begin! If you have completed all 8 assessments ➡ Work-out p.63. If, however, you have chosen to focus on a particular skills area

➡ Managing your work work-out p.67
➡ Managing people work-out p.84
➡ Getting a life work-out p.99.

Work-out

You have now completed your Fitness Assessment, identified your strengths and areas on which you need to work. Now it's time to get fit!

Packed with practical tips, techniques and exercises, Work-out contains all the equipment you need to become super-fit at time management. All you need to provide is your brain and some plain paper to work on.

Look back to your personal fitness profile on p.59. Where do your strengths and weaknesses lie? Do they lie in certain areas of the skill? For example, are you really good at managing your work but poor at managing people? Or do they relate to all three skills areas? Depending on your own fitness profile, you can either focus on improving a particular area of skill or work on individual weaknesses within each area.

Of course, if you want to raise your level of performance in all areas then complete all the activities; then you really will be super-fit.

Work-outs 1-3 relate directly to profiles 1-3. Similarly work-outs 4-6 and 7-8.

The important thing to remember when completing any of the work-outs is that what you do is up to you. And only you can make it work. Much like going to the gym, you have to complete the exercises properly in order to get any benefit out of them. Cheating on the exercises means you won't get the results you want.

Before starting out on the work-outs, remember the top ten time management myths:

Myth 1   *If you have too much work to do you can never get organized.*

Myth 2   *If the job has to be done in a particular way there is nothing you can do to change it.*

Myth 3   *Your job is unique and therefore you cannot apply systems to it.*

Myth 4   *If the system is right you don't need to be self-disciplined to be organized.*

Myth 5   *Your job involves being available for people, and therefore you have to be available all the time.*

Myth 6   *You can't change priorities that are set by the organization.*

Myth 7   *Ordinary everyday jobs do not need to be planned.*

Myth 8   *You can be just as effective if you don't have smart systems such as a clear desk or an efficient filing system.*

Myth 9   *Things will eventually quieten down and then you can get yourself more organized.*

Myth 10 *You are not the problem – it's other people; the organization; the job.*

Managing your work

Managing your work effectively means managing your time. The following three work-outs will help you achieve this.

WORK-OUT 1: ATTITUDE

Your attitude to managing time is largely determined by your experience combined with your expectations and habits. In NLP (neuro-linguistic programming) terms you mentally create a map which represents the world as you see it. It is unique to you and is not necessarily the reality for others, but reality as you see it. This map is formed by your experiences which you use to either reinforce your world-view or to adapt it. If others are expressing a different view to you, you take their view, compare it to your own and if it fits adopt it and if it doesn't you may either adapt your view or reject theirs. So in time management terms, you need to understand what your view is and how it was formed, recognize that others will have a different view which is as real to them as yours is to you and make an effort to change your view if it isn't working for you. This is the beginning of becoming self-aware.

Becoming self-aware

There are three stages to becoming self-aware. You need to have a clear idea of what you want, not just generally in life, but out of any particular moment (even if all you want in that moment is to sit quietly without thinking about anything in particular). You need then to be aware of, and sensitive to, what is going on around you so that you can see what is working for you and what isn't, how you are affecting what is going on and how others are affecting what is going on. Finally, you need to be flexible so that you can change what you are doing or thinking until it does bring you what you want.

What do you want?

What do you want from your life?
On a sheet of plain paper write about yourself as if someone was going to use this material in a speech about your life at

a celebratory dinner. What would you like them to say about you? Try to write it in less than 250 words. Now write about yourself from the point of view of a newspaper critic who is reviewing the speech in the next day's paper, and who has never liked you much. What would they say about you?

Identify the differences between the two descriptions. These differences are your 'plan'. You use them to work out what you need to do in order to achieve the description that you want (presumably the positive one!).

Essentially you have identified some key goals to achieve in order to have the life you want.

What do you want from your work?
Make a list of all the things that you have to do at work, from the most menial to the most important.

Now rate them (1-10) according to how important they are to the job getting done, and how important they are to you. Where the figures match you will probably feel quite positive about the task; where they don't you need to do some work to bring them into line.

Example

Task/Quality	Importance to the job/10	Importance to me/10	Difference
Getting the figures done on time	10	5	5
Producing perfect quality PowerPoint presentations	7	10	3
Responding to post within 24 hours	8	4	4
Producing monthly departmental report	9	2	7

You will now begin to see where there is a discrepancy between what you think is important and what the organization thinks is important. This gives you the basis to make some decisions, such as challenging the need for you to produce a monthly departmental report rather than delegating it.

What is going on around you?

- Stop what you are doing.
- Look at your watch/a clock and make a note of the time.

- Now close your eyes and close your ears and listen to your inner thoughts for a few moments.
- Now open your eyes and write down what you were thinking.

- Close your eyes and listen to what is going on around you for a few moments, making a mental note of the detail.
- Open your eyes and write down what you heard.

- Now look around you and observe what you see, taking a mental note of every detail.
- Write down what you saw.

Your notes might look something like this:

Feeling a bit stressed
Worried about meeting that deadline
Not happy about Michael not ringing when he said he would
Don't know what to do about the missing documents
Can't wait for the party at the weekend
Wonder what to wear

Can hear typing
The hum of the air conditioner
Phones ringing

Can see Joanne speaking to Adam; she looks cross, he looks disinterested

The dried flowers look really a deep, deep blue
The water in the vase has a film of dust on it
The pattern in the carpet looks like a dragon eating a flower

The point of this exercise is to make you aware of the moment. This helps you to stop your mind racing so far ahead that you deal less effectively with the right now. You can do this exercise daily, weekly or at any point in your day when you want to capture the moment and bring yourself back into control.

Who are you – and what can you change?

Under three headings of Physical, Emotional/Behavioural and Intellectual/Interests, write down who you are. Highlight the aspects that you particularly like about yourself.

For example:

Physical	Emotional/Behavioural	Intellectual/Interests
Female	Good sense of humour	Studying for
Blonde	Enthusiastic	psychology degree
Short	Loving	Cricket fan
Curvy	Friendly	Like reading about
Blotchy skin	Short-tempered	science
Curly hair	Get bored easily	Don't keep up with
Small feet	Good contributor	current affairs
Married	in meetings	Love my work
	Hate details	Hate writing reports

Look at the aspects you haven't highlighted. Now ask yourself:

Do I care enough about this to change it?
Can I change it anyway?
If I can, what is my overall goal and what difference will it make to my life?
What do I need to do to begin the change?

This tells you what you are going to do about things that you are not happy with and that you can change, and those things that you are just going to accept.

What do you like?

Take some time to write down what you like about work (eg visiting clients, chairing meetings, doing the figures) and what you don't (eg writing reports, the hours, the boss!). Now identify those things that you *can* do something about and those that you can't; then decide what it is you are going to do about them.

Think positive!

Take a few moments when you first wake up to think about the day ahead. Think of five things that you are either planning to do, or that are going to happen, that you feel good about. They can be anything from a favourite TV programme being on to running your first project meeting.

Now write down three things that you are *not* looking forward to that you have to do or that are going to happen. Think through how you plan to deal with them or what your attitude to them needs to be in order to make them less awful. Now BEGIN THE DAY IN A POSITIVE WAY.

Your attitude to your work directly affects your ability to do it – think positively and remember that you can choose how to think about it. Think of time as a valuable commodity that you choose how to spend rather than as something over which you have no control.

WORK-OUT 2: PRIORITIES

The ability to identify your priorities accurately, in a way that helps you to make good decisions about what to do when, is invaluable. It is essential to effective time management.

Prioritizing simply means ordering things according to their relative importance. So, being able to prioritize means that you know what tasks are most important and need to be done first and/or have more time spent on them/have a higher level of resource or attention.

'Mortgages' and 'new frocks'

Managing priorities involves ('morgage' money) similar principles to managing money. You know what proportion of your salary you need to set aside for essentials, eg the mortgage, phone bills, food etc. You then can play around with whatever money is left to buy luxury items, what I call 'new frock' money. There is also a certain amount of money which is wasted and which you wish you could unspend. I call this 'white elephant' money because you spent it on something you didn't really need and didn't even really want.

Similarly with time, if you can identify your time 'mortgages' (in other words, those things that you absolutely must spend time on to get them done), your time 'new frocks' and 'white elephants', then you are beginning to prioritize effectively.

Make a list of the key tasks in your job. Then, against each one, write down approximately how much time you spend doing it and whether it is a time 'mortgage', 'new frock' or 'white elephant'. In other words, is it essential to be done otherwise you'll get the sack, is it a luxury, or is it a complete waste of time?

Example

Task	Approximate time spent	Category
Writing monthly report	4 hours	White elephant
Completing end of month figures	3.5 hours	Mortgage
Conducting appraisals	2 days	Mortgage
PowerPoint presentations for management meetings	2.5 hours	New frock
Attending weekly team meeting	1.5 hours	New frock

You should now have a sense of what is really important in your job. There may be some things there that you need to challenge yourself on.

Key result areas

Write yourself a completely up-to-date job summary. It should contain the following:

- ✔ A statement of the overall purpose of the job, including its nature and scope.
- ✔ A summary of the key result areas.
- ✔ Under each key result area there needs to be a list of the key objectives for each one.
- ✔ A description of the essential tasks contained within the job, setting down clear job responsibilities which need to be carried out in order for the key objectives to be met.
- ✔ A statement of reporting lines and accountabilities.

Once you have written this down, take it to your line manager to see if they agree with what you have written. Amend it accordingly.

This should be revisited and updated every 6 months.

Prioritizing when in doubt

Sometimes it isn't immediately apparent what the priorities are, especially if you are faced with a mountain of tasks, all of which seem to need immediate attention. In these circumstances, the tasks can always be broken down into one of four categories: important and urgent, important and not urgent, urgent but not important, neither urgent nor important. Make a list (overleaf) of the immediate tasks that face you and then complete the grid.

Immediate tasks

....
....
....
....
....
....

Important & urgent		Urgent & not important	
Important & not urgent		Not urgent & not important	

Do those tasks that are important and urgent first, urgent and not important second, important and not urgent third, and don't do the not urgent and not important ones at all if you can get away with it!

Eating toads

Sometimes you are faced with two tasks of equal importance. In this case you can use the 'two toad' technique, courtesy of Mark Twain.

Mark Twain has a story about eating two toads. The thought of eating two toads is disgusting. This means that having eaten one we probably don't much fancy eating the other one. If we eat the small one first, the thought of then eating an even bigger one is going to make it hard to do. However, if we eat the big one first, the smaller one won't seem quite so bad. It's the same with hard tasks. Tackle them first, get them out of the way, and any subsequent jobs won't seem so bad.

So, to decide between conflicting priorities of equal importance you simply need to decide which is the bigger toad and eat that one first.

Example

1   Finish monthly operating statement

Big toad

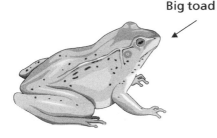

Produce tender for client

2   Little toad

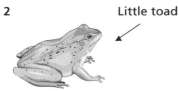

Rolling 'to do' list

For this exercise you will need either an A5 diary, a 'to do' facility on your computer or an A5 hardback book with each page dated.

A rolling 'to do' list involves planning as you go along. Essentially, either in your diary, the A5 hardback book or on your computer, every time you think of something that needs to be done you write it down on the day on which you intend to do it. For example, if you suddenly remember that you need to write to Gary at Head Office, but not until the 13th (and today is the 2nd), then turn to the 13th of the month and make a note. You can then simply forget about it, because when you open the page dated the 13th you will be reminded that you need to write to Gary because it is written there. Do this with every task, including personal ones. If, for some reason, you can't do the task on that day, simply move it to a day on which you can do it.

WORK-OUT 3: TASKS

Having simple and effective systems to help you manage tasks makes a big difference to how well you are able to maintain a positive attitude, where you essentially feel in control and at the same time deliver on your priorities.

Most of us in work are inundated with paper, e-mails, voice mails and all the other paraphernalia of working life. However, there are some simple techniques and systems which can help us cope.

Traitorous trays

Get rid of those trays! Rearrange your desk so that you only have two trays on it. The first tray should be clearly labelled 'In' and the other tray 'Filing'.

The 'In' tray needs to be emptied at least twice a day, and it needs to be in a prominent position where people can see it. Make sure that it is obviously empty; that will encourage people to put incoming work into the tray rather than onto your desk.

The filing tray should be emptied at least twice a week. If you are super-fit, however, you will file paperwork every day.

TRAINER'S TIP

Do your filing first thing each day when you feel fresh and motivated.

Proactive and reactive time

Proactive tasks are those tasks that you can plan for, that you know are going to happen. For some tasks, such as opening the post, you can't anticipate the content, but you do know you will have some actions as a result. For others you know what they are and how long they will take.

Reactive tasks are those tasks that you couldn't, or didn't, plan for, and that often involve a disruption to your day.

This exercise will help you identify how much of your time is spent on reactive tasks and how much on proactive.

Over the course of the next working week, make a note of every task that you do, how long it took and whether the task was reactive or proactive. You can either do this by completing a daily time log, as illustrated below, or simply by listing the task and the amount of time and making a note of whether it was proactive or reactive.

Example of a daily time log

Time begun	Activity	Total time taken	
0907	Arrived at work – got myself a coffee – chatted to Rose	11 minutes	R
0918	Began to open post	6 minutes	P
0924	Interrupted by Mark asking about TMF	8 minutes	R
0932	Back to post	1 minute	P
0933	Came across letter, needed to ring client immediately		R
0933	Rang client – not in, left message to call back	2 minutes	R

Time begun	Activity	Total time taken	
0935	Back to opening post	12 minutes	P
0947	Interrupted by phone – accounts calling re JP expenses	15 minutes	R
1002	Back to post	13 minutes	P
1015	Client returned call	23 minutes	R
1038	Back to post	9 minutes	P
1047	Began work on report	12 minutes	P
1059	Interrupted by boss re meeting	17 minutes	R
1116	Back to report	15 minutes	P
1131	Went to make coffee	5 minutes	R
1136	Back to report	22 minutes	P
1158	Interrupted by phone – Lee re Tim	14 minutes	R
1212	Back to report	18 minutes	P
1230	Went to lunch with team		P

You can see from the above example that out of a total morning's worth of time (3 hours and 23 minutes in this case), 1 hour and 35 minutes were spent on reactive tasks and 1 hour 48 minutes on proactive tasks.

Of the proactive tasks, 41 minutes were spent on the post and 67 minutes on the report. So, although these two proactive tasks only totalled 1 hour and 48 minutes they actually took 3 hours and 23 minutes to complete because of the interruptions.

This is a fairly typical example of how proactive time is disrupted by reactive time. So from now on, when planning tasks, you need to take into account the interruptions.

In this case it's roughly 50:50 proactive:reactive, therefore this individual needs to plan double the amount of time to complete proactive tasks (unless you can guarantee not being interrupted).

You need to work out your own average percentage.

You are now ready to begin diary planning.

Diary planning

For this exercise you will need a diary (paper or electronic).

This exercise is ongoing. Essentially, the idea is that you use your diary to make appointments in, not just appointments to see people or go places, but also appointments to carry out tasks, in particular tasks that are likely to take you half an hour or more. You don't need to plan every minute, but give yourself enough time to complete the tasks.

Having completed the reactive/proactive exercise, you should now have a rough idea of how much time to allow for reactive tasks. For example, if you plan to do something that takes an hour and your proactive:reactive ratio is 50:50, then you need to allow two hours in which to do it.

> **TRAINER'S TIP**
>
> *Never go anywhere, especially to a meeting, without taking your diary.*

Make a list of all your tasks, no matter how small. Then estimate how much time they will take you to do. Factor in your allowance for reactive tasks and then put all of them into your diary, choosing sensibly which day on which to do them. Don't allocate them for sooner than you need to because you won't do them, you'll keep putting them off to the deadline. But do remember to give yourself a clear day between completion of the task and the deadline in case something major goes wrong (eg the computer breaks down!).

Include personal things and keep it all in *one* diary!

You can see from the example overleaf that there has been plenty of time allocated for reactive time.

This system can be used in either a paper or electronic diary system. If people can see you regularly using and updating your diary they are less likely to plan in meetings without checking with you first.

The 'everything book'

An 'everything book' is simply an A4 or A5 book (usually hard backed) in which you write absolutely everything, from notes

Example

	Monday	Tuesday	Wednesday	Thursday	Friday	Saturday	Sunday
0900	Gen admin	Gen admin	Gen admin	Project meeting	Dentist		
1000	Team meeting	OSC report			Prepare OSC presentation		
1100				Finish OSC report			
1200					Pub with team		
1300	Lunch	Lunch PM	Lunch				Lunch Anna
1400	Start OSC report		1-1 PB	Do expenses	Finish end of month figures		
1500		Begin end of month figures	Research LBT	Prepare 'awards' mailmerge	Meeting WH		
1600		Phone Alec Stewart	1-1 GW				Back to London
1700			Deb leaving-do				
1800					Drive to Exeter		
1900							
2000	Meet Rose				Dinner with Brad	Summer Ball	

of meetings to scribbled phone numbers. You keep successive books for as long as you need to and you only ever need to look in one place.

Fight the filing

Most of the filing we do is a complete waste of time. There are very few documents that we actually need to keep. The originator will always keep a copy. For this exercise, every time you are considering filing something, ask yourself the following questions:

1 What is the worst thing that could happen if I threw this away?
2 Who else will have a copy?
3 Is there a legal requirement that I keep a copy?

As a general rule of thumb, you should not need to file more than about 10% of all the paperwork you receive. If you have scanning facilities then scan in documents that you don't need paper copies of for legal reasons. Otherwise, the rule with filing is the three R's.

> Read
> Reply
> Reject (ie THROW INTO THE BIN! Preferably the recycling bin!)

With filing systems the trick is to keep things simple. Colour coding different kinds of files helps, eg blue for management meetings, red for financial information, yellow for projects etc. Then keep to a simple alphabetical system. Don't file anything that doesn't absolutely need filing.

With electronic filing systems, again the trick is to keep it simple. Avoid folders with general titles like 'letters' etc. Try to split your folders by topic, just as you would a paper-based filing system. Similarly, if you are typing a letter, memo or other document that doesn't need to be saved, then delete it. You don't need to clutter up your PC's memory with rubbish. Plus, the more clutter in there, the slower your machine will be.

Make sure that you do a header or footer for every document which lists which folder the document is in and what you called it. Make sure that you keep your file names specific to make them easier to find. For example, *Letter to bank* isn't a good name because you will probably write loads. However, *Bank letter re overdraft facility – Oct 2003* is much more specific and will make it easier to find. Additionally, you will be able to tell what is in the file simply by looking at the name without having to open it every time.

TRAINER'S TIP

Don't make up permanent files for things you are working on. Use jellies to keep the paperwork in and file in the 'bring forward' system. When the work is complete, chuck away any paperwork you don't need; only file the essentials.

Dealing with paperwork and electronic mail

Again, this is a very simple exercise.

By following the simple set of rules below your paperwork problems will be minimized.

1 Deal with paperwork at the same time every day.
2 Treat e-mail just as you would any other paperwork.
3 Don't flick through the pile of paper to scan what's there or skim the headings of e-mail – deal with each thing as you touch it or open it.
4 When you read it, make a decision according to the following flowchart.

Paper or e-mail–action required?

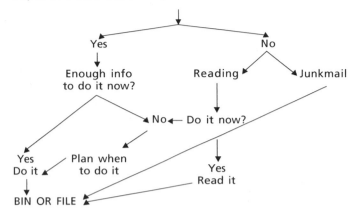

Managing your work checklist

✔ Your attitude to work directly affects your ability to do it – think positively and remember that you can choose how to think about it.

✔ When in doubt about priorities, prioritize, 'important and urgent' tasks first, then 'urgent and not important'.

✔ When faced with two equal priorities, do the bigger task first.

✔ Only keep two trays on your desk – the 'In' tray and 'Filing'.

✔ Do your filing first thing each day.

✔ Factor in time for reactive as well as proactive tasks.

Managing people

People are time-consuming! They waffle on, butt in and don't listen. They make mistakes. How you handle people affects your ability to get your job done well, and time effectively. The following three work-outs will help you establish your personal best method of working with people as well as giving you some hints about how you might improve your approach.

WORK-OUT 4: PEOPLE

To be effective at dealing with other people (no matter what the issue is or whom you are dealing with), you need some basic skills.

The people pleaser

On a sheet of plain paper make a list of the qualities or behaviours you think your friends would say you have when dealing with people. Now do a list of the qualities or behaviours you think your enemies, or people you have upset, might say about you.

What you will probably find is that the lists are complementary. In other words, where you put 'honest and open' for your friends, you may have 'blunt and rude' for your enemies.

Essentially, for many of us, the things we think we are good at when dealing with people might be perceived differently by others. Their perception is formed by our behaviour towards them combined with their own thinking about who we are. Learning to recognize how others might see you in a negative light will help you manage your behaviour in a way that will support you in your relationships.

> **TRAINER'S TIP**
>
> *For extra knowledge, ask a friend or a good colleague to give you feedback on what you do well, and what you do less well, when dealing with people. Make sure you listen and don't try to explain yourself.*

What is my 'already always listening'?

When we listen to other people we are never actually listening with a 100% open mind. We are 'already always listening' – we have already made some conclusions about them from the way they look, sound and anything we have heard about them. We are also making a judgement about whether we already have a view on what they are saying. Finally, our mood also affects how we hear them.

Essentially, we listen with the three E's – our Ears, our Eyes and our Emotions. We bring to our listening all of our prejudices, biases and experiences which create a filter through which others attempt to pass on their messages. And the same is true of people listening to us.

Make a list of some of the things which may influence how you listen to people. Note whether they will make you listen positively or negatively.

Your list might look something like this:

~ Like people who wear suits
~ Switch off as soon as anyone makes a sexist remark
~ Don't like scruffy hair – I think it means people have low standards
~ Don't like people who drone on and don't get to the point
~ Accountants are boring
~ Men who wear jewellery are sleazy

To find out how strong your 'already always listening' is, try practising on a friend. Ask them to give you their view on something that you disagree about. Listen, paying careful attention to both what they are saying and how it makes you feel. Don't interrupt them. At the end, summarize to your friend what you thought they said and see how accurate you are. Also tell them how you felt about what they said and discuss how that affected your ability to listen.

Another good exercise is to listen to a piece of news, or a programme on the radio or television, that activates emotions in you. At the end of the piece make a note of how you were feeling, and how that affected your ability to listen openly. Then try to explain the piece to someone else, taking the opposite view to the one you would normally take, and see what happens.

Getting to know other people

A sure-fire way to get co-operation at work is to get to know the people you work with, not just in your own team or department but further out in the organization.

Make a list of people you would like to know better. Choose people from different departments, especially those with whom you have dealings. Over the course of two weeks, find out the answers to the following questions about them.

TRAINER'S WARNING

You need to be genuinely interested in getting to know people to make this work. If you fake it, they will know and you  *may damage relationships irreparably.*

TRAINER'S TIP

Don't ask all the questions at once, and watch your body language.

1. What do you enjoy most about your job?
2. What is the best book you have ever read (or what are you reading at the moment)?
3. What music do you like?
4. What is your pet hate?
5. Who would you want to play you in the movie of your life and why?

6 What did you want to be/do when you were a child?
7 What do you like least about working here?
8 What do you like most about working here?
9 What can I do to help make your job easier?

This is just a suggested list of questions which touch both on people's personal lives (without being intrusive) and how they feel about work – which is the most relevant to you, of course. Feel free to find other questions which suit you better.

Dealing with people when things go wrong

This is a simple exercise which you should complete every time you are faced with having to deal with someone because they have missed a deadline, made a mistake or done something wrong.

There are two steps to this exercise.

Step 1 – be sure that you are *acting* rather than reacting

Stop: assess the situation, think about what your 'already always listening' is
Look: at the other person; what are they telling you through their body language and expression?
Listen: without prejudice; what are they trying to tell you?

Step 2 – state what you want, and how you feel, constructively

Say:
When you … (do/say/act)
I feel/X happens … (the consequences of what they do or say)
In future/next time I'd like … (whatever it is you want them to do differently).

> **TRAINER'S WARNING**
>
> *Be careful not to get into blaming or asking the other person to explain themselves. They will nearly always have a reason, valid or not, and getting into arguments about why something happened doesn't help to move it forward. The keys to success in this exercise are avoid* *blame and focus on the future.*

Meeting people in other departments

The following tips will help you create and maintain relationships with people in other departments.

✔ Visit people in their own departments.
✔ When arranging meetings, you go to them.
✔ Once or twice a week deliver internal messages face to face.
✔ Whenever you go into another department, make an effort to speak to someone.
✔ Thank people for everything they do for you, no matter how small.
✔ If someone from a different department comes to yours, make an effort to say hello and exchange a few friendly words.
✔ Find out exactly what other departments do and what their priorities are.
✔ Regularly ask other people what you can do to improve your support to them.
✔ Attend social functions.

Just say No

Write down a list of things that you have said Yes to in the last few weeks. Then go back over the list and write down what you wish you had really said. Now re-write what you wish you had said in a way that makes it inoffensive to people and yet still leaves you without the job/commitment!

Example

Agreeing to do Lisa's report	I'm always doing your work – do it yourself this time.	I am happy to have helped in the past, however, I can't continue to help out as I have my own work to do. Sorry, but No.
Agreeing to go to Phil's party	God No! Your parties are always so boring.	Thank you for the invitation, however, I cannot come.

Remember, when saying No:

✔ Don't be deliberately unhelpful – offer alternatives if you can.

✔ Briefly and clearly state what you are *not* willing to do followed up with a statement about what you *are* willing to do, if appropriate.

✔ Don't make profuse apologies.

✔ Offer an explanation if necessary, but avoid over-justification.

✔ Keep it short and simple.

✔ Avoid personalizing your refusal.

✔ If pressed, repeat your refusal, slowing down and stressing important words.

WORK-OUT 5: MEETINGS

Many people feel that meetings are a waste of time. However, meeting people is one of the ways in which we get our jobs done, regardless of whether the meeting is formal and pre-arranged or *ad hoc* and impromptu. The main reason why people dislike attending meetings is because they are badly run; attendees go off the point or pontificate endlessly while others don't say a word. Often it's not clear what the purpose of the meeting is or what it has achieved.

Clearly, having a good Chair in a meeting makes all the difference, however, you can't guarantee that.

These exercises assume that you are not the Chair at the meeting; they will help you to make the most of even the most badly run meeting.

Deciding which meetings to attend

Draw up a checklist of criteria which need to be fulfilled for you to agree to attend a meeting.

TRAINER'S TIP

Don't make the criteria unrealistically stringent or you'll end up missing important meetings or invalidating your checklist by attending them even if they don't meet all your criteria.

You may want to weight some of the criteria, so that some outweigh others, or you may want to specify a minimum number which need to be fulfilled. A suggested checklist is below – but you will probably need to invent your own, or add some more categories in order to make it completely relevant to you.

Question	Yes	No
Do I know the purpose of the meeting?		
Is there an item on the agenda which is fundamental to my work?		
Is there something in my work which I need to share at this meeting which cannot better be done some other way?		
Is there a piece of information I may learn at this meeting that I cannot find out any other way?		
Am I required to attend because of my position at work?		
Will my non-attendance adversely affect the ability of someone else to complete their work?		

If the meeting does have an agenda, and not every item is relevant, then only attend for the items that are relevant to you. (Explain this to the Chair and outline what work you'll be able to complete instead.) If the agenda isn't timed then ask at what time the item will be and arrive about five minutes before (just in case they are running ahead). You can then leave immediately after.

You could even ask for the item to be timed at a particular time that suits you.

Preparing for the meeting

In order to get the most out of any meeting, before attending make sure you:

✔ Get the agenda.

✔ If there isn't one, ring up the person holding the meeting and ask for one.

✔ Clarify the purpose of the meeting, either from the agenda or the Chair.

✔ Read the agenda as soon as you get it so that you can establish if you need to do any preparation.

✔ If the agenda doesn't specify in enough detail what an item is about ring up the Chair or the person whose item it is and ask.

✔ Do whatever preparation you need to, including reading any paperwork that has been sent out to you prior to the meeting.

Below is an example of a good agenda. Encourage people to use something along these lines.

Example

Agenda:	Team Meeting, 20 April 2003
Venue:	Goodwin Room, Turner House
Time:	2.00pm to 4.00pm
Attendees:	Debra Tyler, Lisa Allcock, Paula May, Vincent Cooper, Will Rimmer, Kath de la Pole
Purpose of meeting:	To report on activities to date and decide priorities for the next month

Time	Item	Who
2.00	**Introduction** and restate purpose	DT
2.10	**Update on department finances**	VC

A report on progress – please read the operating statement in advance

Team updates   **All**

Three minutes each from each team on key developments

1   Lisa
2   Paula
3   Vincent
4   Will
3.00   **Product Z**   LA

Update on development of product Z and request for help in selling

3.20   **Telephone project**   WR
       Presentation on options. Decision as to which
       supplier to go with. Final agreement on budget
3.45   **Summary and actions**   DT
4.00   End of meeting

Expressing your views

Some people have difficulty expressing their views in meetings; others seem to go on forever! The following tips will help you ensure that your views are relevant and timed. This will also give you some confidence to speak out if you are a little reticent.

✔ Prior to the meeting jot down any questions you have thought of relating to items on the agenda.

✔ Make sure you sit where you can clearly see (and be seen by) the Chair and others in the meeting.

✔ During the meeting (as people are talking) jot down what you are thinking and what questions have occurred to you.

✔ Indicate your desire to speak by attracting the attention of the Chair (raise your hand).

✔ Make your point succinctly. Don't be tempted to over-explain.

✔ Then shut up and listen to the reply.
✔ Don't allow people to interrupt. If they do, raise your hand (palm towards them) and say 'May I complete my point?' or words to that effect (without being rude, obviously).
✔ At the end of your item summarize, if necessary, what people have said.
✔ If you think that people are getting off the point, remind them of the time and the agenda item.

Taking notes

You shouldn't rely solely on the minutes to remind you what meetings were about or to prompt you to complete your actions. However, taking notes does not mean you are actually taking minutes, it simply means that you are jotting down things that strike you as you are listening to them and making a note of your own actions.

One of the best ways of doing this is to produce a 'pattern note' rather than taking linear notes.

Example

> **TRAINER'S TIP**
>
> *Use appropriate body language and tone of voice, even if you are asking someone to stop interrupting or get back to the point. Keep your comment light, and smile wherever appropriate so that people don't feel rebuked but reminded.*

> **TRAINER'S TIP**
>
> *Highlight actions to distinguish them at a glance from general notes.*

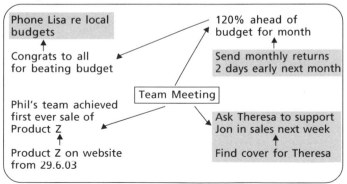

Phone Lisa re local budgets

Congrats to all for beating budget

Phil's team achieved first ever sale of Product Z

Product Z on website from 29.6.03

Team Meeting

120% ahead of budget for month

Send monthly returns 2 days early next month

Ask Theresa to support Jon in sales next week

Find cover for Theresa

'Meeting bingo'

This is a fun, light-hearted game to make meetings more interesting and also to highlight the use of unnecessary jargon.

'Meeting bingo' rules

✔ Make up bingo sheets for everyone in the meeting.

✔ Pick jargon words or words that are used a lot in your organization which you want to stop using (eg 'At this point in time', 'It's not my job to do that' etc).

✔ Each player gets a sheet and has to cross off the word when s/he hears it.

✔ The winner is the player who first completes their sheet.

> **TRAINER'S WARNING**
>
> *Make sure you don't play 'meeting bingo' in a way that's offensive to individuals in the meeting or could cause offence of either a sexual or racial nature.*

After the meeting

To make sure that you don't go to future meetings without having carried out your actions:

✔ Immediately after the meeting spend 10 minutes going through your notes and planning when you are going to complete your actions, using the diary planning system or the 'bring forward' system.

✔ Do those actions that are quick and easy immediately (eg if someone asked you to send them some information).

✔ Make a note of information you need to pass on to your colleagues or the rest of your team and think through the best way to do it – eg by e-mail, an *ad hoc* get together or your own team meeting.

WORK-OUT 6: INTERRUPTIONS

Handling interruptions is a crucial part of successful time management, but it is a skill that many of us have to work on. The thing about interruptions is that they usually involve other people. The combination of a desire to please and be helpful with a feeling of guilt if we are not available to people makes it very difficult to say No or to send people away.

Having said that, interruptions can often be self-inflicted. We interrupt ourselves.

What to do when people interrupt you face to face

People will normally interrupt you face to face because they want to ask you a question or ask you to do something. You have a choice; you can either stop what you are doing and deal with the interruption straightaway or ask people to come back at a time that is more convenient for you.

The trick is to handle the interruption in such a way that they feel you have been helpful, but you have minimized the interruption. If you can deal with it quickly then do so. Otherwise try saying something along the lines of 'I want to be able to give you proper attention for this. Could it wait until X time so that we can talk properly?' Or 'Can I think about it and get back to you at X time?'

Finally, try to manage your time so that people are interrupting you when you are prepared to be interrupted.

Check out the following tips:
- ✔ Encourage people to check in advance what time is convenient for you to see them.
- ✔ If someone pops in to see you, and you can't politely tell them to go away, stand up when you are talking to them. This will discourage them from sitting down and getting comfortable and will cut short the interruptions.
- ✔ In extreme cases, pick up some paperwork and make as if you have somewhere to go. This will encourage them to get to the point quickly.

✔ Don't get involved in chat if you haven't got time. If someone does want to make small talk, use humour to point out that you are busy.

✔ If you need to see someone, go to their place of work rather than having them come to you. That way you retain control of when you leave.

✔ Don't be an interrupter yourself. Get into the habit of checking with people if it is OK for you to talk to them now. This habit will then rub off on others.

Dealing with telephone interruptions

The telephone is the most common form of interruption. The main problem is that we assume that we must deal with the phone immediately, and others assume that because we have answered it then we have the time at that precise moment to deal with them.

The following tips will help you manage the telephone:

✔ Make telephone appointments. Tell people specifically what time you intend to call them, or ask them to call you at a specific time.

✔ If you are asking someone to call you back, give them a specific time when you are available.

✔ Learn the facilities of your phone, such as conference call, ring back, call waiting etc.

✔ When phoning people make it clear in the first 30 seconds what you are phoning about and how much time you are likely to take; then ask if this is convenient for them.

✔ Make a telephone agenda before you call to make sure you are covering everything you need to.

✔ Keep a note of actions agreed in your 'everything book'.

✔ Use standardized telephone message forms and encourage others to do the same.

✔ Use message boards so that when people come into the office they can immediately see if there are messages for them, or, if they phone in, others only have to glance at the message board to see if there are any messages.

Creating time to think

Keep a record of your interruptions (see below). This will help you identify who interrupts you the most, or what is the most common cause of your interruptions. You will then be able to analyze your record and see if there are any patterns.

Who	What about?	Start time	Finish time	Total time

Once you have analyzed your record you may well notice that there are periods of time where you are more interrupted than at other times. My advice would be to go with the flow here. Make yourself available to be interrupted at those times, and plan to do the sort of work that doesn't require detailed, undisturbed concentration during those times.

Mark out two different kinds of time in your diary; time when you are available and time when you would prefer not to be disturbed. Make it clear, both in your own personal diary and your office diary, which the two times are and let people know (if you have an electronic or computer diary which people can look in even better). On the whole you will find that they stick to the times.

Why not suggest this approach to all of your team so that everyone gets a chance to work undisturbed?

Handling crises and fire fighting

If you are finding that you are having to handle too many crises and put out too many fires, one of the first things that you need to do is find out what's going on.

For every crisis make a note of the following:

1   What was the cause?
2   Who was involved?
3   How long did it take to sort out?
4   Could it have been avoided?
5   What could you do to avoid it happening again?

Get into the habit of using this simple crisis checklist:

✔ Before reacting, stop and think. Keep calm and ask yourself 'What is the first best step to take to minimize the fall-out from this crisis?'
✔ Don't assume something is a crisis immediately. It may Others may be over-reacting. The calmer you are, the calmer they will be and the less it will feel like a crisis.
✔ If you find yourself stressing about the crisis, take some time to put it into perspective before doing anything. Ask yourself, 'What is the worst thing that can happen?' Then, 'What is most likely to happen?'
✔ Check out the facts before acting. Do you have the info you need to deal appropriately with the crisis?
✔ Think about who else you need to involve – only involve those who really need to be involved.
✔ As you are dealing with the crisis, make a note of any systems or procedures that need to either be improved or put in place in order to deal with a crisis next time.
✔ Remember that a crisis can be turned to your advantage. At the very least there is an opportunity to learn and improve in some way. You may even be able to impress the customer/your boss/colleagues by how you handle it.

Managing people checklist

✔ Be aware of your 'already always listening' – ie what prejudices you bring, and judgements you make, when listening.
✔ Get to know people you work with, both in your own team/department and beyond.
✔ When things go wrong be careful to avoid blaming; focus on the future.
✔ Prepare for meetings – and take notes.
✔ Make it clear to other people times when you are available and times when you would prefer not to be disturbed.

Getting a life

The following two work-outs will help you achieve balance, and minimize stress. They will help you get a life.

WORK-OUT 7: BALANCING LIFE

Having balance does not mean that everything is equal. What it simply means is that you feel that you are giving the right amount of time and attention to any given aspect of your life. Clearly, your life cannot be in balance at all times. There will always be occasions when for one reason or another you are having to spend more time at work or at home. This is normal; the important point is to ensure that you eventually redress the balance.

My life cycle

Write down all the things in your life that are important to you. Now draw a circle (see example below) and divide it up according to how much time you are spending on each. Then draw another circle and divide it into how you would like it to be. Now check out the difference between the two 'pies'. Write down what you need to do to resolve these differences.

My life now

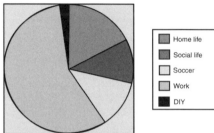

How I want it to be

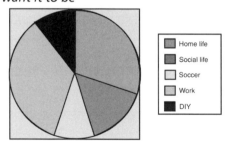

Chores

Many of us spend a lot of time doing chores at home. Sometimes we spend so much time doing chores that we actually miss out on the most important priorities. This is especially true if you are a bit of a perfectionist around the house. You can spend so much time doing DIY or housekeeping that you find you are not spending quality time with your children, friends, partner etc.

To work out if you are spending the right amount of time doing the right things at home, make a list of all the jobs that you do and how much time they take you each day/week.

Example

Job	Time taken
Washing up	15 mins per day
Vacuuming the whole house	1 hour a week
Cooking	45 mins per day
Washing	2 hours a week
Household shopping	1.5 hours a week

Now add up the number of hours you have at home (include the time from when you get up until when you leave for work and then from when you get home to when you go to bed).

For example, if you get up at 6.30 and leave for work at 7.45 and get home around 6.30 and go to bed around 11.30 you have 6 hours and 15 minutes of 'home time' during the week.

Then see how much of that time is taken up by chores, and how much you spend on mindless activities such as watching television. (I am not saying that you shouldn't watch television. However, if you make a note of how much time you spend doing that rather than talking with your partner or playing with your children you might get a bit of a shock.)

For example:

Time	Task
06.30	Got up, got ready for work
7.00	Made breakfast while watching breakfast TV
7.20	Put a wash in
7.30	Woke the kids up
7.45	Left for work
****	At work
6.30	Got home, showered and changed

Time	Task
6.45	Went to supermarket
7.30	Got home, made dinner
8.00	Ate dinner while watching TV
9.00	Programme finished, washed up, chased the kids to bed
9.20	Rang Sam for a chat
10.00	Did a bit of work for tomorrow
11.00	Watched the late news
11.15	Went to bed, read for a bit
11.45	Fell asleep

This is just an example, but hopefully you get the picture. By analyzing where you are spending your time you may begin to make different choices, or try different ways of doing things. For example, could you get everyone to do the chores together so that you are both getting the job done and spending time together? Could you afford a cleaner?

And remember, what is more important, an immaculately tidy house or a slightly untidy house because you spent time with the children or your partner? Don't let the style in which you live your life get in the way of *how* you live your life.

Communicating your needs

It is important that you are able to explain to people, both at home and at work, what is going on for you and what you need in order to get your life in balance.

Ask yourself the following questions:
1 What is going on for me in my work-life balance right now?
2 What do I want to happen?
3 What do I need to do to make it happen?
4 Who do I need to tell about what I am doing?
5 Who can help me to make it happen?

Then get going by working out what it is you need to do and talking to the appropriate people about it. Find out what others need to help them achieve balance.

Playing the 'I have to' game

Many of us get into poor time habits. That is to say, we do things simply because we have always done them, ourselves, in that way, at that time and to that standard.

To play the 'I have to' game, first write down all the things that you think you have to do.

Then get someone to challenge you on what you have written, asking you the following questions:

1 Do *you* have to do this?
2 Do you *have* to do this?
3 Do you have to do *this*?

If the answer to any of the above questions is Yes, double check by asking yourself:

1 Why do I have to do this?
2 What would be the consequences of not doing it?
3 What will I gain by not doing it?

WORK-OUT 8: MANAGING STRESS

Stress is essentially a term used to describe the pressure that is being put on us, either internally or externally. In itself it is not a bad thing and, in fact, a certain amount of stress (or pressure if you prefer) is actually essential to life. You must have noticed that when you are operating at a level of optimum stress you are busy and feeling challenged but at the same time feel that you are able to cope; you feel in control, positive and creative.

It is when we are experiencing too much challenge (or, more importantly, when we *perceive* we are), combined with feeling that we do not have enough support, that problems occur.

Stress is different for different people. What causes you to feel stressed will not necessarily be the same thing that causes someone else stress. Additionally, we all have different symptoms of stress.

Identifying the things that cause you stress

There are five main generic causes of stress:
1 Our perception of the demand placed upon us.
2 Our perception that there is no balance between the amount of challenge and the amount of support.
3 One bit of our lives is either taking up more time and attention than it should, or another bit isn't getting enough time and attention.
4 We are asked to do something that challenges our values.
5 We are experiencing a period of major change.

For this exercise make a list of all the activities in your life that are causing you stress ('stressors'); then rate them out of 10 for the level of stress, with 10 being the highest. Then determine, according to the grid below, whether you can do anything about these stressors. If you can, decide what you need to do, if you can't, decide what you can do to minimize the stress.

Example

Stressor	Score	Can I fix it?		What do I do?
		Yes	No	

For the 'What do I do?' answer, you may find that completing the other exercises in this work-out will help you manage the action you have decided to take, or be clearer about what to do.

Dealing with the problem

For any stressor there is normally a cause or an event, which may or may not be within your control. The first thing to do is see if you can remove the cause of the stress. Do remember, however, that the symptom is not the same as the problem. For example, if you are struggling with a particular job at work you may be missing deadlines not because you have too much to do but because you haven't been trained properly. This simple flowchart should help you identify the difference and deal with what you can.

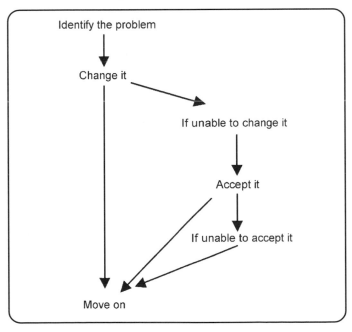

Changing the way you see the situation

As mentioned earlier, for many of us stress is more about how we interpret the situation we are in than the situation itself.

When you are feeling stressed do the following:
1 Write down the thing that is causing you stress.
2 Write down how it is making you feel.
3 Then write down how your behaviour is being influenced by the stressor and your feelings.
4 Now ask yourself the question: What is the worst thing that could happen?
5 If that worst thing happens, what can you do about it?
6 How likely is it that the worst thing will happen?
7 What is the most likely thing to happen?

Completing this exercise will help you put things into perspective. Things are rarely as bad as we think, and we nearly always have the skills and abilities to deal with most of what life throws at us.

These are a few of my favourite things

Sometimes the stress is being caused by worrying about the problem or the situation. You need to identify those things that you can do that will take your mind off the situation. This is called 'active distraction'.

Make a list of all the things you like doing that will help distract you. Put them into priority order (ie those you would do first, then if that didn't work what you would move on to).

Example
1 Read
2 Cook
3 Watch TV

4 Go for a walk
5 Take some exercise
6 Work in the garden.

These are a few of my favourite people

During times of extreme stress, it is important that you are not over-independent or self-reliant. Talking to someone about what is bothering you can often help you to see the wood for the trees and put things into perspective. Bottling up emotion rarely helps, and usually exacerbates your stress.

This exercise is about building up your support network. Bear in mind that it is unwise to rely on one person to fill all your emotional needs. No one person can realistically fill all our needs and by relying solely on one person you can put too much pressure on the individual or on your relationship with them.

Identify your support network by completing the following.

Question	Name
Who can I rely on in a crisis?	
Who makes me feel good about myself?	
Who can I be totally myself with?	
Who can give me honest feedback in a way that I can accept?	
Who can I talk to when I am worried about work?	
Who can I talk to when I am worried about home?	
Who is able to make me stop and think about what I am doing?	
Who helps me to put things into perspective?	
Who is good fun to be with?	
Who helps me to take my mind off things?	
Who introduces me to new ideas, people, opportunities?	

Gaining control in a moment of stress

If you are immediately faced with a moment of stress and you need to gather yourself back together, try out the following exercises.

Thinking of nature
Go to a window or a door with glass and look outside. Look for a piece of nature that is particularly attractive – a tree, a flower, a piece of grassland. If you are indoors, perhaps a plant. In an emergency, close your eyes and imagine something.

Focus on it. Look for the tiny detail. Notice the colour, the shape, the sounds if there are any. Notice how it fits in with its surroundings. Imagine the forces of nature that created it.

Going to a quiet place
Close your eyes and imagine that you are walking through a door. Outside the door is a large field full of tall waving grass. You are walking through the grass, the sun is shining, there is a gentle breeze. On the other side of the field is a place that you think of as being peaceful and safe. Imagine what it is like in detail. Then imagine yourself going and sitting there and letting calm wash over you. When you have recovered yourself, go back through the field and through the door and then open your eyes, keeping that sense of peace and calm with you.

These exercises are great for quickly regaining your equilibrium so that you are better able to deal with a stressful situation.

Getting a life checklist

✔ Be aware of what you are spending your time doing. Know how much time you want to spend on various activities.

✔ Tell other people what you need to achieve balance.

✔ When managing stress make sure you are dealing with the problem not the symptom.

✔ Ask yourself: What is the worst thing that could happen?

✔ Deal with the problem if you can, or accept it, but don't worry about it.

Keeping Fit

Keeping Fit

Congratulations on finishing the book. Hopefully you have enjoyed the experience and gained from the advice and insights offered.

As you have discovered, the ability to manage your time effectively is the key to freedom. It means you are more cheerful, less stressed, produce better quality work and have more time to spend with family, friends and, of course, yourself.

But like any skill, practice makes perfect and the more times you use it the better you get at it. You need to keep skills fit, and this is what the final part of this book is all about ...

Keeping fit

Managing your time effectively is a vital skill, and it is important you don't let it slip.

You need to keep on your toes, keep practising. If you feel your skills slipping then look through the book again, remind yourself of the key learning points, even run through a couple of exercises. Better still, set yourself some real-life targets *now* to keep yourself up to scratch. These could be anything from going out and buying an 'everything book' to saying No to an imposing colleague.

Make a note of your targets in your personal fitness plan below (bearing in mind the benefits it will bring you, or others). Specify actions and time-scales; this will keep you focused and fit.

Personal fitness plan

Target/Action   By when   √

....

....

....

....

....

....

....

....

....

....

....

....

Further Reading

Further reading

Allcock, Debra, *Time and Workload Management*, The Industrial Society/Spiro Press, 1995

Carnegie, Dale, *How to Win Friends and Influence People*, Pocket Books, 1994

James, Judi, *Bodytalk*, The Industrial Society/Spiro Press, 1995

New, George, and Cormack, David, *Why Did I Do That?*, Hodder & Stoughton, 1999

BFS

B